PENGUIN

OFFICE SECRETS

Harish Bhat, currently the brand custodian at Tata Sons, has held many roles in the Tata Group over the past thirty-five years, including as managing director of Tata Global Beverages, and chief operating officer of the watches and jewellery businesses of Titan Company Ltd.

An avid marketer, Harish has helped create several successful Tata brands. In 2022, *Forbes* listed him as one of the world's top ten most influential chief marketing officers. He writes extensively and is a columnist for *The Hindu BusinessLine* and *Mint*. He has authored five books. In 2019, LinkedIn selected him as one of their top voices in India.

Harish is an incorrigible foodie and fitness freak. His wife, Veena, is a data scientist. They have a daughter, Gayatri, who has embarked on her professional career. Harish can be reached at bhatharish@hotmail.com.

Celebrating 35 Years of
Penguin Random House India

PRAISE FOR THE BOOK

'When does a manager become a human being? Well, to my mind, when they meander into anecdotes about their family and friends in the middle of a desperately boring meeting, or when they talk about, say, a kachoriwalah in Jaipur to illustrate an innovation. When they have the courage to call a consultant's often-repeated point "a wide ball".

If you want a detailed understanding of the points I have made, please read Harish Bhat's *Office Secrets*. You will love it like I did'—Piyush Pandey, chairman of Global Creative and executive chairman (India), Ogilvy

'Harish Bhat's *Office Secrets* will make you laugh out loud, warm your heart and nourish your intellect, all at once. He unravels the daily joys and mysteries of modern work life with insight, humour and grace. This accessible compilation of his popular column has a universal appeal for every office-goer—from a management trainee to the CEO'—Aparna Piramal Raje, bestselling author of *Chemical Khichdi*

'This book is full of fun and insightful observations on corporate life. Business professionals tend to take their craft too seriously and Harish Bhat punctures that corporate ego with his illuminating, incisive, never over-the-top or crossing-the-boundary sense of humour. Reading this book will make you wonder, "Is that me Harish is talking about?"'— Shiv Shivakumar, operating partner, Advent International

'I really enjoyed reading this book as it shines a light on everyday ordinariness. As life gets bigger, the small things grow more important, in a wry paradox.

One of the things Harish is reminding readers through these pages is that while the world can be often complex and confusing, it can also be motivational and meaningful. The stories truly celebrate office life in all its beauty and irreverence as well as help us better understand our place in the world'—Sohini Roychowdhury, chief, Marketing and PR, UNICEF – Private Fundraising and Partnerships Division

'Nuggets of wisdom in every byte, wrapped in corporate everyday experiences that are so easily relatable too. Harish's treasure of reminiscences, beautifully distilled, is such a delightful read for everyone! Come, enter the world of *Office Secrets*!'—Hema Ravichandar, strategic HR advisor and former global HR head, Infosys

'*Office Secrets* brings forward such nuanced and thoughtful observations on office life that it seems much less dreary and almost delightful! Tiny but terrific hacks to navigate corporate corridors are peppered liberally in this gem of a book and I had many a chuckle to myself as I resonated with Harish's gently humorous essays'—Suparna Mitra, CEO, Watches and Wearables, Titan Company Ltd

Office Secrets

50 Human Truths You Should Absolutely Know

Harish Bhat

**PENGUIN
BUSINESS**

An imprint of Penguin Random House

PENGUIN BUSINESS

USA | Canada | UK | Ireland | Australia
New Zealand | India | South Africa | China

Penguin Business is part of the Penguin Random House group of companies
whose addresses can be found at global.penguinrandomhouse.com

Published by Penguin Random House India Pvt. Ltd
4th Floor, Capital Tower 1, MG Road,
Gurugram 122 002, Haryana, India

First published in Penguin Business by Penguin Random House India 2023

ISBN 9780143462484

Typeset in Adobe Garamond Pro by Manipal Technologies Limited, Manipal

www.penguin.co.in

To the late R.K. Krishna Kumar,
a legend of the Tata Group, who taught me the
office secrets of hard work, kindness and generosity

Contents

Introduction   xiii

1. Why Do People Talk So Much during Meetings?   1
2. Why Being Generous Is an Essential Trait of a
   Great Leader   6
3. The Cookie Club   10
4. Six Rules That Marked Working from Home   14
5. Tired of Being Tired? Go Ahead, Hit the
   Refresh Button   18
6. Have You Spotted the Balloon in Your Office?   22
7. Why Daydreaming Is a Good Thing   27
8. Why Writing Makes Us Happier   32
9. A Beginner's Guide to Recovering from Meetings   37
10. Dump the Slides; Add Power to Your Point   41
11. New Laws of the Digital Workplace   45
12. Your Office Companion Spills the Beans   49

13. Do You Ask Questions That Really Matter?   53

14. Make February Your New January   57

15. Listening: A Vital Managerial Skill   62

16. Pandemic Habits We Should Stick To   67

17. Tune into the Blues to Work Smart   72

18. Finding Hotspots for Ideas   76

19. What Your Wall Says about You on a Video Call   80

20. The Joy of Using a Notebook   84

21. Hercule Poirot Can Solve Your Work Problems, Too   88

22. Please Add Kindness to Your To-Do List as Well   92

23. Old-School Charm at Work   97

24. What If Working from Home Goes on Forever?   101

25. Seven Habits of Very Happy Managers   105

26. What the Dickens?   110

27. An Office Worker's Guide to the Zodiac   115

28. How Often Do You Praise Others?   119

29. Conference 101—and Ways to Add Some Fun   123

30. Monsters Inc.   128

31. The Geronimo Effect at Work   132

32. And the Office Oscar Goes To . . .   136

33. PERM Yourself in Office   141

34. Mathematics at Work   146

35. Meet Shakespeare, the Manager's Guru   151

36. Become a JEDI   156

37. Einstein on the Job   160

38.	What to Wear, When	165
39.	For Your Next Offsite, Opt for Offbeat Destinations	170
40.	The Art of ACE-ing Your Office Conversations	174
41.	SOAR above the Job	178
42.	Time to Think	183
43.	What Your Cubicle Says about You	188
44.	Horseplay at Work	193
45.	The New-Age Boss	198
46.	Coffee, Matcha or Coconut Water?	203
47.	What Should You Do When You Fly?	208
48.	New Principles of Our Office Lives	212
49.	Taking Note of What Is Said	216
50.	How Do You Look during Meetings?	220

Epilogue	225
Acknowledgements	229
Notes	235

Introduction

Do offices have secrets waiting to be discovered? Can these secrets help us become more effective managers?

The answer is a resounding YES. Offices hold plenty of powerful and useful secrets, though not of the kind you think. These are not secret financial numbers or confidential strategy documents hidden away in locked drawers or in safes. Instead, they are simple secrets present all around us. Yet, we do not often see them.

This book offers a selection of fascinating and useful secrets that can help you be far more successful at your workplace. As a bonus, they can make you happier as well.

Let me tell you a few stories that exemplify the kind of secrets I am talking about. Some of these stories are fictional and pieced together from years of assorted observations, so please do not ask me if these specific people actually exist, but do believe me when I say that the lessons they teach us are totally real.

Gopal's Secret of Generosity

Let me begin with a true story. It was almost ten years back that I decided to write my first book. I work with the Tata Group in India, and I gathered the courage to request an appointment with a senior director of the organization, R. Gopalakrishnan, a well-known writer himself. I wanted to request his guidance on what I should write about. I knew him only remotely at that time and was unsure whether he would be able to give me time amid his hectic schedule. But to my pleasant surprise, he replied promptly, agreeing to meet me.

Gopal gave me over an hour of his time, to discuss the theme of my book and the specific stories that would feature in it. Later, when I was writing the book in the library of the Tata Management Training Centre in Pune, he came across to the centre, spoke with me and ascertained how my book was progressing. He also agreed to read the entire manuscript and write the foreword to the book.

In doing all this, he taught me a secret that many great leaders and managers know and practise—the secret of generosity. He was generous with his time and suggestions. He has similarly helped several other colleagues and friends. No wonder so many people I know go to him for advice and respect him greatly. Gopal is an expert in many areas of management, but it is his generosity with dispensing his expertise that makes him stand apart.

Suresh's Secret of Recovery

I have a colleague called Suresh*. He and I have sat through so many meetings together. Meetings of all kinds. Happy

---

* Not the real name. I have used this fictional name to represent one or more people whom I have come across, who have demonstrated this behaviour.

meetings, sad meetings, delightfully crisp meetings, infinitely long meetings. And we have also endured many painful and bad meetings, including some where we were pulled up severely, and others where long PowerPoint presentations were followed by important-sounding but totally useless discussions. You can say that ours is a kinship of meeting-induced suffering.

I would feel terrible after such meetings, and it would sometimes take me a full day to recover. Sometimes I would carry my funk with me into the next discussion. But I found that Suresh always quickly bounced back to his normal, ebullient self. *How does he do this?* I thought to myself. And so, I observed him closely for a few weeks.

I found that after every bad meeting, he would vanish for around half an hour. On following him a couple of times, I discovered that he would go out for a nice walk around the office block all by himself, stopping by for a cup of tea at a nearby place. When I asked him about this, he taught me the secret of thirty minutes of me-time, which helps one recover incredibly well after a bad meeting. 'Be by yourself,' he told me. 'In fact, think of some of the ridiculous points of the meeting and smile. Reflect and let go. Only half an hour, but it restores your mental balance and your soul so well.' I have tried Suresh's secret recipe and it has, without fail, helped me swiftly bounce back to my productive best.

Noella's Secret of Asking Questions

Whenever Noella* is in a discussion, she excels at sparking off the right conversations, which have often led the team to great

---

* Ibid.

new insights and brilliant ideas. She somehow achieves this even when she is not an expert on the topic at hand. This is not a one-off occurrence; I have noticed it time and again. Others have noticed it too, I think, because she gets invited to several important discussions.

I realized that her secret was in the art of asking the right follow-up question at the appropriate time. For instance, a colleague would have just delivered a presentation on a subject, say, on building stronger brands using the power of social media. Noella's hand would promptly go up. She would ask a question regarding a specific point the speaker had made about engaging followers on Facebook or on Instagram. The speaker's face would immediately light up because that topic was right up his alley. His response would then take us into deeper conversation on how exactly to build viewer engagement, leading to a very meaningful and relevant discussion.

In addition, these follow-up questions have also made Noella a popular person, because she is perceived as a good listener and one who is responsive to the thoughts being tabled. I have tried practising Noella's secret in many meetings and it has inevitably worked very well.

Jai's Secret of Filter Coffee

Whenever I have visited Jai's* office for a meeting, I have always come out happy. I have been there several times. Sometimes the meetings have been very useful. At other times, the discussions

---

* Ibid.

have not been so satisfying. Yet, every time, my happiness quotient has increased post a visit to Jai.

The reason is very simple; he serves excellent South Indian filter coffee in his office. It is steaming hot, golden-brown, frothy yet of thick consistency, as good filter coffee should be. It has just the right proportions of coffee and chicory, creating an unbeatable blend of aroma and strength.

I am told that a local coffee-making expert has taught the staff at Jai's office pantry how to make superb filter coffee, though I have never specifically asked him about this. But I am shameless in saying that I love going across to his office because I quite look forward to the coffee. This is Jai's secret of making his visitors feel special, and it gives them one more reason to say a quick yes to his requests for formal and informal meetings. (Here again, I have desisted from using Jai's real name, lest there be a stampede outside his office. Let his name and location remain a secret for now.)

Harish's Secret of Daydreaming

For a final tale of how office secrets help us, I turn to a true story about myself. Often, when I am wrestling with a challenging problem and a solution continues to elude me for several hours or days, my mind gets saturated and no new thoughts emerge. To tell the truth, I feel a little lost. In such moments of despair, I turn to a secret that I discovered many years ago. I indulge in some daydreaming. I daydream about vacationing on the beaches of Goa or trekking in the Himalayas or eating my favourite fish and chips in an English pub. I daydream about dancing the night away with friends or watching the stars frolic in the skies on a clear night.

When I do this, something magical happens (though, to be honest, this happens sometimes and not always). A penny drops somewhere, I hear the distant clink and a possible solution to the problem I have been grappling with appears right in front of my eyes. Here it is, a Eureka moment. I don't know how that happens, but it does. Daydreaming is my own little secret. So, let no one tell you that daydreaming is a waste of time.

Everyday Secrets

Pause here for a moment. Reflect on the five stories you have just read and the secrets they have revealed.

1. Generosity
2. Thirty minutes of me-time
3. The right follow-up questions
4. Filter coffee
5. Daydreaming

These are diverse subjects, for sure. Moreover, these are not the typical workplace secrets or methods that we are taught in business school. Yet, they are very effective, because they are built on human truths.

Truth be told, we are all human beings at heart: regardless of whether we are mighty chief executives, powerful finance managers, or somewhat tentative sales interns. We may study and practise the latest marketing strategies or digital techniques, we may attend important seminars or conferences in impressive-looking pinstriped suits, but in the deepest corners of our heart, we are greatly moved by things such as sheer generosity, or a steaming cup of coffee offered with love and care.

Such are the subjects that this book contains. The fifty essays you will read in the following pages will reveal and discuss these everyday secrets. You will find within a range of subjects—whether the best methods of fighting exhaustion, organizing your work desk, the power of listening, why kindness is so important, workplace lessons from Hercule Poirot and what you can learn from the cookies that your colleagues eat.

Some of these topics will delight you, others will provoke you by raising new questions in your mind, a few may even amuse you. Some essays are irreverent in their tone and others are reasonably serious. Yet, in all of them, you will find a light touch reminding us not to take our corporate avatars too seriously.

Regardless of what your specific emotive reactions are, I am confident these essays will leave you with fresh thoughts. New ideas on how to enhance your professional effectiveness in the office. Simple suggestions on how you can make a larger positive impact on the people around you. Some interesting concepts that can potentially trigger new joy or even a bit of happy consternation at your workplace. That is indeed the primary purpose of this book—to provide you new thoughts and ideas to toss around and use as you wish.

May I make a final point, before I leave you in peace to leaf through these pages? The topics covered in this book are not in any pre-arranged order. While I have written these essays over the past ten years, the topics which they cover have no chronology or expiry date. You are therefore welcome to dip into these essays at your leisure and in any sequence that you wish, and their relevance will not be shaken. That is the good thing about these fifty office secrets: they are timeless, and you can discover them whenever you wish to.

1

Why Do People Talk So Much during Meetings?

There are many motivations at play in the office, ranging from attention-seeking to compulsive rambling.

So many meetings in our workplaces last for so long because people talk too much. I have a hypothesis that if participants in a discussion listened more and spoke up only when they had a really important and relevant point to make, most meetings would be over in less than one-third the time they currently take. Unfortunately, because people have so many motivations for speaking at meetings, lots of us will continue to speak often and at length unless these underlying urges are suitably addressed.

I have endured thousands of such meetings in my thirty-year career, and it is highly likely I have also made others to endure me as well (I do speak a lot). But these sessions have given me a small silver lining—they have helped me develop a system to categorize people who speak at meetings.

I present these archetypes below in the hope that this understanding may sensitise us and set us on the path towards shorter, crisper discussions.

The Attention Seeker

Here is the first type, who is often seen. This person speaks primarily to catch the attention of their boss, or senior people attending the meeting. They believe that being heard by the top brass ensures visibility. So, they will pipe up at least once during each meeting. Content is of secondary importance. They may merely echo a point made earlier by someone else, albeit packaged in a different way to appear original. Or they may make a brief point unrelated to the subject of discussion, but of general interest, such as an inane observation on the weather that morning.

The Compulsive Speaker

This person loves to hear his own voice. He is not really speaking to impress anyone in attendance but is rather following his calling in life, which is to speak. He will launch into long commentaries on the subject being discussed and, if he's the presenter, you can expect impressive monologues accompanying each PowerPoint slide. You may think he has finally finished speaking, only to discover that he has merely taken a pause. The length and dominance of his contribution determines his satisfaction with the meeting.

The Witty Soul

She looks for every opportunity to exhibit her wit and elevated sense of humour. Wit and humour, when used in moderation, can prove to be effective tools for breaking the monotony of a meeting or lightening up a tense situation. However, repeated interjections can prove irritating, regardless of how humorous they are. But this does not deter the witty soul. She believes that she has an obligation to treat the audience to her intelligent puns and clever acerbic comments, and that they will love her for it.

The Know-It-All

Mr Know-It-All prides himself on his vast knowledge of all matters under the corporate sun. He speaks mainly to showcase his extensive knowledge to the people gathered around. He often reels off cryptic facts and figures to support his interjections, and there's no certainty that anything that he says is accurate or even relevant to the topic at hand. He seeks to impress, and you may even hear him name-drop authors, philosophers and their ilk, as sources from where he has drawn his wisdom. His presence in a meeting is likely to significantly extend its duration.

The Mighty Critic

Here is a person who revels in being critical of every idea that is presented. She knows how to pick holes in virtually every suggestion and will speak mostly to tell everyone why something cannot work. It is not that she works overly hard at being critical, it is just that this behaviour comes naturally to her. When she feels that she has thoroughly demolished an idea, she is at her happiest. The mighty critic is unlikely to ever offer an original idea of her own, perhaps because she has already killed it in her own mind.

The Rambler Bambler

He rambles in a disjointed fashion, trying to articulate an idea that has emerged from the recesses of his mind. However, he takes a long time to do so. His thoughts meander through the foliage only to return to where he first began. At other times, he begins to speak even before the idea is yet to fully form in his mind. This leads to varying degrees of beating around the bush. He is generally well intentioned, but brevity is not his forte.

Quiet Contributor

Here is a person who listens carefully and silently for most of the meeting, and speaks briefly only when she thinks she has something meaningful to add. Sometimes, she is so quiet that the head of the meeting or others present must encourage her to speak. Here is a rare species, and perhaps the sort of person we all love to include in a meeting. The problem is that Mr Compulsive Speaker and Mr Know-It-All hardly allow her a chance to speak.

The Silent Type

Finally, I have come across people who attend meetings but do not say a word. They are totally silent, and I wonder why they are there. Yet they are being invited to meetings all the time, and they are clearly fine with joining, because I see them there. Often, they take extensive notes too. I am intrigued by these participants. Are they spies? Have they been granted observer status? Have they taken a spiritual oath of silence? I do not know.

The only positive point here is that they do not contribute to extending the length of meetings.

I love narrating stories during meetings, which are at times tolerated and at other times ignored by colleagues.

2

Why Being Generous Is an Essential Trait of a Great Leader

Generosity is not charity. It is an act of reaching out to our colleagues and signalling to them how important they are to us.

Many years ago, when I was working at Titan, I was keen to write my first book, themed on the Tata Group. I requested a meeting with R. Gopalakrishnan, who was then the executive director of Tata Sons. He was one of the seniormost leaders of Tata Group, and an accomplished author himself. I wondered if, given his busy schedule, he would be able to meet me at all.

To my surprise, he gave me more than an hour of his time. He asked about the theme of my book, why I wanted to write it, and also the specific stories that could feature in it. When I was writing my book at the library of the Tata Management Training Centre in Pune, he came there one weekend to ask how things were progressing and offered some suggestions. And, finally, he read the entire manuscript and agreed to write the foreword to the book.

It was very generous of him. He offered a lot of encouragement to a rookie writer like me and shared his expertise freely, all in the midst of a busy calendar. The support helped me publish my first book and start my writing journey.

This episode also made me realize how generosity is a wonderful trait displayed by so many great leaders and wonderful colleagues. Generosity is not charity. It is an act of reaching out to our team members or peers and signalling to them how important they are to us. It is an act of kindness that is incredibly motivating to the receiver and equally fulfilling to the giver, and it, thereby, creates even stronger bonding and team spirit within organizations.

How can we practise everyday generosity within our workplace? Here are a few thoughts on this subject.

Listening and Sharing

Generosity comes in many forms. We can show generosity by listening to our colleagues with respect and empathy, instead of rushing through a conversation because we want to get on with work, or multitasking on the phone during a chat. This requires investment of time and conscious effort, but when a person feels that someone is truly listening to them, they feel valued. This, in turn, can enhance their motivation and productivity.

Generosity is also about sharing all essential information readily. We need to resist the urge to hoard information because this signals selfishness to everyone around and hampers team spirit. We are drawn to leaders who share essential information with us quickly, tell us where things stand and what is likely to come up soon. Leaders possess this information because they have access to networks and perspectives that we may not have.

Another great way to show generosity is to publicly share credit wherever required, and recognizing and appreciating the contributions of team members. All this requires is mentioning their names during a meeting, or an appreciative email. One of my colleagues is particularly good at this, and I find that his team members are far more eager to contribute, even in challenging situations. The need for authentic recognition of our efforts is ingrained in all of us.

All about Giving

Generosity is also about ensuring reciprocity in our professional relationships. So many of us are experts at the hustle, totally focused on getting what we need from our colleagues and from other teams. While this may be necessary, we should also consider how much we are giving back to them.

Give time to help brainstorm ideas for someone else's project, give opportunities by opening doors or providing contacts, give expertise to help a young team member, give a friend who has received poor feedback a shoulder to cry on. As leaders, when we give generously, we also set the norm for the behaviours we wish to see in our teams.

Doing the Unexpected

Sometimes generosity is about creating delight by doing far more than what is expected, or even doing the unexpected.

I recently had the opportunity to meet the legendary cricketer Kapil Dev at the 2022 IPL finals. I went up to him and asked him for a selfie to send to my sister, who is such a big fan of his that she has saved every single press clipping of his matches.

Kapil Dev took me totally by surprise. Instead of merely obliging my request for just a selfie, he went ahead and recorded a personalized video message for my sister on my phone—a small, generous gesture by an icon that my sister will cherish forever. The workplace provides us many such opportunities to create memorable experiences for our colleagues. If Kapil Dev can do it, why can't we?

True generosity is about being gracious to people regardless of whether they are our peers, our juniors or even strangers. On the other hand, being super nice to our bosses to please them while being close-fisted with our team members does not count as being generous.

A final word. Generosity does not mean compromising on the quality of work. Not at all. In fact, it is an essential leadership trait in any workplace that wishes to achieve sustained world-class excellence. This is because great performance requires people with great motivation, and generosity is one of the key factors that makes our spirits fly.

I acknowledge the generous inputs received from my colleague Suparna Mitra of Titan, which have made this piece possible. I have learnt from her that generosity is also about readily giving your time for a conversation with a colleague, without glancing down at your Titan watch every now and then.

3

The Cookie Club

We must never underestimate the potency of the humble cookie and what it can tell us about our colleagues.

Organizations are becoming increasingly worried that their employees are losing the battle to Continuous Partial Attention. For a few years now, texts and emails have become irritating but addictive distractions during important corporate discussions. But there is a silent enemy far more potent than beeping devices—the humble cookie.

I recall a meeting where the chief executive had just unveiled his brilliant new strategy—the bold acquisition of an unsuspecting global competitor. The audience, a select group of twenty top managers, was captivated by this daring approach. But unfortunately, at that very moment, the cookies were served. The platters placed on the table contained plump coconut cookies, chocolate-chip biscuits and a rare but immensely appealing blackberry variety. The attention in the room shifted immediately from the CEO's presentation to the china platters, and for some time the only acquisition on the managers' minds was laying their hands on the cookies before they vanished.

I don't immediately remember whether that strategic plan made headway. But the cookie platters were certainly polished off, the meeting never quite recovered its flow and twenty contented managers left the conference room soon thereafter. The cookie had struck.

Companies must, therefore, never underestimate the potency of the humble cookie. Don't even call them humble because the varieties served in today's conference rooms range from the amazingly delicious to the incredibly exotic. Within these cookies reside irresistible and dangerous temptations, including blackberries, cashew nuts, almonds, hazelnuts and flavoured creams. Bombshells that never miss their targets.

While managers uniformly greet the arrival of cookie platters at meetings, their responses vary and are most educative to observe. Here is my 'cookie classification' of managers based on several years of sharp observation.

At the top of my list is the Grabber. He identifies his favourite cookie and grabs it as soon as the plate is plonked on to the table. Since assorted platters are often designed to contain only one each of a type, his reactions are lightning-fast. He spares no thought for his compatriots and their possible choices, nor is he concerned about whether others will look askance. This man has absolute clarity on what he wants in life and will waste no time getting there. Indeed, his philosophy finds both its origin and destination in Ayn Rand's belief that selfishness is the ultimate virtue.

Close behind is the Vacillator. This man finds it difficult to choose between the cashew-nut cookie, the chocolate chip and the simple Marie biscuit. He loves them all, yet he has the civilized decency to know he must take only one at a time. So, he vacillates, and even turns over a couple of the cookies endlessly in an effort to choose. Finally, he picks one under some internal duress. Here is the man who will forever be dissatisfied with his life choices and will live a life of constant regret. A sort of brooding Hamlet of today's cookie-filled corporate world.

Then we have the Health Fanatic. To him, a cookie is primarily a source of empty calories and cholesterol. To begin with, he absolutely resists the temptations placed before him, even pushes the plate away. If he is famished, he will eventually break off a tiny piece of the least dangerous cookie and chew on it meditatively. Then one more piece, and one more, until he finally decides it's not really worth leaving the last wedge behind. This 'zero-sum' consumption fitness hero, whose life is a constant struggle in a fat-obsessed society, leaves the meeting resolving to eat less at dinner.

Let's not forget the Picky Eater, who believes that only some parts of the cookie are really worth eating. He will pick out and eat the chocolate chips or the cashew nuts from within the biscuit, leaving large craters behind. Sometimes, he has the shameless audacity to actually open up a cream biscuit in full sight of the entire meeting, and pick out only the delicious cream, leaving a cream-less ruin behind. This man is most likely to pick and choose his way through life, a road inevitably filled with long waits, ecstatic moments and disappointments.

This brings us to the Civilized Sacrificer (CS), a personality type which comes to the fore when the last cookie is left on the plate. He will eye this constantly but is convinced that eating the last one is not the civilized thing to do. So, he will sacrifice his cookie needs and wait endlessly until another colleague eventually eats the piece, at which point he experiences an internal moment of triumph. The matter becomes complex if he is surrounded by others like him, in which case the last cookie remains perennially untouched. Expect this man to surrender the last taxi of the night to a passerby, or to prioritize the demands of his friends. A nice guy to have around, particularly if you want to cadge a cigarette or borrow some money.

And, finally, the Carrybag. He believes that cookies are meant to be taken away and not left behind. At the end of the meeting, he will silently pocket a few of the remaining cookies; if possible, all of them. He may slip them into his laptop bag or bundle them into his handkerchief. He may stuff them into his pockets. His conscience is in the clear, as he believes his company has already paid the hotel or conference hall for these cookies. Such a person believes in a maximizing approach to life, one where he will claim every last penny he perceives is due to him, either fully or even marginally. A wonderful negotiator to have on your side.

These few 'cookie classifications' illustrate how deep this subject goes, and how distracting it can be. So, some enlightened organizations are simply considering a change in strategy—replacing biscuits with roasted peanuts during their board meetings. That's the way the cookie crumbles in today's corporate world.

I drool endlessly over cookies that have lots of pineapple cream and a glob of jam in the centre.

4

Six Rules That Marked Working from Home

As most of us finally head back to office, some irreverent reflections on the past few years of WFH.

After nearly two years of continuously and intermittently working from home during the pandemic, I returned to working from the office in 2022. I love working out of an office; I think it makes me much more productive. In addition, nothing can substitute the insights and joy I gain from impromptu conversations with colleagues I meet down the corridor.

But the extended WFH period, like all other situations, had its own unique charms, exigencies and humour. Here is a quick look at six irreverent but real rules that marked the WFH period.

The Mute and Unmute Theorem

The word 'mute' took on new meanings during all our WFH zoom calls. In particular, the phrase 'You are on mute' stuck with me, even appearing in my dreams!

Despite my best efforts, I often end up being on mute while speaking, at which point my colleagues pounce on me with great relish. However, it's not too long before some other disturbance arises on the call and I hear an instruction—'Can all of you go on mute?' This is an excellent illustration of Newton's Third Law: every action has an equal and opposite reaction.

The Distractions Hypothesis

This hypothesis states that the probability of a new distraction turning up every day during WFH is close to 100 per cent. The origins of such distractions are varied—social media, binge-watching, online shopping, gaming, kids, pets, wilting plants, assorted couriers turning up at the door amid conference calls and seeking OTPs with great urgency, frantic attempts to restore home WiFi or a sudden ruckus from the home next door. A corollary to this important hypothesis is that it is impossible to predict most such distractions. Still, you can only ignore them at your peril, so it is best to reconcile with this reality and adjust everything else accordingly.

The Twenty-Four-Hour Rule

This rule defines an important human truth—that it is very difficult for two people to spend all twenty-four hours together every day, for two years at a stretch. You may be deeply in love with your partner or spouse and totally inseparable as a couple, but day-long observations of their work idiosyncrasies, constant shop talk and general sloppiness can sometimes be too much to handle. This is particularly true when both of you share a single room or dining table for working from home. This rule makes you realize that working from separate offices has one unintended benefit—it has held many relationships together.

Goa Envy Axiom

Here is an axiom that was applicable to most of us during the WFH period. Each of us knew at least one friend, colleague or acquaintance who decided to move to Goa and work from there during this time. Goa can be substituted with the Himalayas, Lonavala, Alibaug or even the Bahamas, depending entirely on the type of people in your professional or social circles. Those of us who stayed on had many reasons why we did not relocate to the beaches or mountains. Eminently logical and hardworking reasons they may be, but they didn't help with the envy. Each time the guy in Goa appeared on a video call, you thought of yourself and what could have been.

The Intellectual Look Postulate

Video backgrounds matter on Zoom calls, and if you want to be perceived as an intellectual type, then there is only one easy solution—you need books in the background. It does not matter if you have not read any of these books, if they are fresh from the bookstore or even borrowed from your neighbour. What matters is the sheer number of books and how weighty they look. An entire library shelf behind you, packed with volumes, is an unbeatable visual for sure. And if you throw in a few well-known authors who write thick philosophical tomes that are seldom read, your intellectual gravitas is guaranteed. On the other hand, a neat background with flowers and pictures on the wall speaks a very different language.

The Children and Pets Maxim

This maxim involves a belief in extra-sensory perception. It tells us that if you have small children or pets at home during WFH, they figure out exactly when an important work-related call begins and turn up magically at that time to assist you with the call. This holds true regardless of how remotely they are located before the call begins. They could decide to help by appearing dramatically in the camera frame, starting some sort of typing on the keypad of your laptop computer or cleaning up your table by getting rid of the coffee mug you have placed there in one fell swoop. They also deploy many other techniques of well-intentioned helpfulness, which are too numerous to list here.

My favourite axiom is based on the unfortunate observation that our appetite for snacking goes up significantly while working from home.

5

Tired of Being Tired? Go Ahead, Hit the Refresh Button

Two years of Covid-19 have created multiple sources of fatigue for many of us. Here are some ways to fight the exhaustion.

So many conversations during the aftermath of Covid-19 are about tiredness. Two full years of the pandemic created multiple sources of fatigue for many of us. A colleague who loves being around people told me how the isolation of working from home had tired him out. Unfortunately, his office, which had reopened for a few weeks, shut down again because of the third wave of the coronavirus. A friend spoke about her elderly mother, who underwent a bout of Covid illness, post which she turned increasingly cranky and irritable. As the primary caregiver who also had to deal with the pressures of the pandemic, my friend was feeling fatigued too.

Then, there are conversations about online learning fatigue being faced by our children and Zoom fatigue that has become par for the corporate course.

Under such difficult circumstances, it is important to be sensitive and kind when we engage in these discussions. But many of us have reached a crossroads where we realize that we are actually tired of being tired.

Talking about illness, isolation and loss saps us of our positive mental energy. It requires significant stamina to commiserate or empathize when this becomes a recurring subject of conversation, though we may genuinely feel the pain at the other end of the line.

And yet, our roles at home and in the office require this of us. So, how do we counteract all this talk of consistent tiredness? How can we un-tire ourselves and bring as much happiness and peace as possible into our busy lives?

Of course, adequate nutrition and sleep are essential for our health and well-being. These topics have been covered in detail by any number of health and wellness experts. However, this is not enough as a lot of our perceived fatigue originates within and dwells deep in our minds. We also need to do other things regularly to rejuvenate ourselves.

Talk, Talk, Talk

A good way to start is to engage in positive conversations with colleagues, family and friends. There are some people who are naturally positive and optimistic, regardless of the circumstances. Maximizing happy conversations with them can drive our fatigue away. We need to initiate positive subjects of conversation wherever and whenever we can.

Conversations about something creative, interesting or beautiful, such as the hibiscus blooming in your terrace garden, or the Hyderabadi chicken biryani you ordered for lunch last weekend, or how an important office presentation came together superbly despite the challenges of collaborating remotely—such conversations can bring a moment of joy in your life, even if momentarily. Don't wait for positive conversations to occur naturally, take the lead and set the tone yourself.

It is likely you will emerge invigorated at the end of the discussion.

Laugh Often

Creating occasions to laugh a little, every day, is a great antidote to fatigue. Laughter lightens the mood and boosts energy levels. Some people are natural humourists and even serious meetings take on a happy tone when they are around. The rest of us can also try our hand at sparking some laughter, without worrying too much about our little jokes falling flat.

Try narrating a humorous incident from your own life or see the funny side of office work. There is a lot of this around, if we only care to look for it. Laughter at the dining table is another great opportunity, though this generally requires collective meal occasions without the distracting clutter of mobile phones and laptops.

Exercise Is Always a Good Idea

While working from home, I have found that getting off my chair and taking even a small brisk walk helps release my happy hormones. The more sedentary I am, the more listless I feel. This is particularly true of office workers like me, where a lot of time is spent in front of laptops and phones. Staring at a computer screen for several hours a day is a definite recipe for fatigue. A brisk walk inevitably restores my mental strength, and a short outdoor walk in the sun does that even better.

And Go Ahead, Do Nothing

We can also 'untire' ourselves by doing absolutely nothing for some time every day. Resisting the urge to engage in that one final task for the day when you are feeling the onset of tiredness, or switching off from the challenging environment around you by listening to music, or merely sitting in that favourite corner at home—all these help us create 'do-nothing' spaces, which can refresh our minds. There was a pre-pandemic time when I would sometimes feel guilty about doing nothing. But not anymore, and certainly not in these times. We owe ourselves the happiness that it can inject into our lives.

I untire myself by writing, and I think the ability to benefit similarly is perhaps true of every creative pursuit.

6

Have You Spotted the Balloon in Your Office?

An exploration of the many varieties of balloons that float around our workplaces and what we can learn from them.

There was a time in 2023 when balloons suddenly became the flavour of the season. A famous Chinese balloon floated across the American skies for nearly a week before it was eventually shot down by the US defence forces. Reportedly, one more such balloon hovered somewhere over Latin America for some time.

Then, there was the short-seller company named after Hindenburg, the famous balloon airship which had burst into flames several decades ago. This company and its balloon-inspired name gained sudden and dramatic fame in India for a brief period, after it published a report that received wide coverage.

Closer home, in an episode fraught with much less geopolitical or economic implication, two helium balloons of unknown origin—one pink and the other yellow—floated into our bedroom. These were presumably from a birthday party in the neighbourhood, though this fact was never conclusively established.

My wife was quick to dispose of them because it is rather disconcerting to have a balloon hanging around over our bed. While this was simple enough to accomplish for a person as determined as my wife, it is not easy to dispose of all the balloons that float around in our offices. Here are some of them for you to think about.

Floating a Trial Balloon

Sometimes, when we wish to test our colleagues' reactions to an idea or a proposal we may have in mind, we initially float a trial balloon to observe their reactions. Such a trial balloon may consist of a tentative or limited announcement or query. For instance, if an offsite meeting is in the offing, one of the organizing team members may trigger an innocuous discussion in the larger group about the relative merits of Paris, Miami and Goa as conference destinations. Sometimes organizations may consider an intentional news leak of an upcoming product to assess consumer opinion and then progress development of the product only if the response is favourable. This is a trial balloon too. Experts in this sphere (I am so sorry for this pun) know how to package the trial balloon smartly so that it floats in very smoothly and without encountering any suspicion. We must learn from them.

Hot-Air Balloons

We know these people, don't we? We meet them in our offices, and they talk and talk all the time. You could call them hot-air balloons (HOBs) but they are also called gasbags, which is really the same thing if you think about it. The hot air that emanates from them carries little substance, but you can feel your head getting increasingly hot and humid as you exercise your utmost patience in listening to them. Mostly, they talk because they are compulsive speakers, but other motivations may include a deep-seated need for attention or an underlying desire for fame. The subject of conversation is of no consequence to them because they are happy to speak about anything. A HOB I know well can wax eloquent about sales techniques in rural India, Mexican bullfighting and Japanese dinner etiquette without really saying anything at all about any of these topics. It is best to keep a safe distance from hot-air balloons lest they burst all over you.

Going Over Like a Lead Balloon

Recently, at a late-evening meeting, I narrated a joke to some of my colleagues in an attempt to project the funny side of myself. Immediately after the narration, I waited eagerly for the laughter, but there was none. Everyone remained rather glum and serious, and then got ready to go home. Clearly, my joke had gone over like a lead balloon. This is, unfortunately, the sorry tale of many submissions and proposals in our offices, which die as soon as they are born because no one likes them or considers them worthwhile. It is also the tale of many new projects and product launches, which fail miserably because they are poorly conceived and go down like lead balloons. But we should take heart from the story of a famous music group who were told that they, too, would go down like a lead balloon. One of the members of the band took inspiration from this phrase and named the group

Led Zeppelin, after the famous airship balloons called Zeppelin. They became one of the best-known rock groups of all time. So, don't ever get discouraged; lead balloons can fly high, too.

Pricking His Balloon

If you have a pompous boss or team member in your workplace, then you are possibly fed up of listening to their tall stories and constant self-praise. This sometimes leads to a desire to prick their balloon. Many office-goers are adept at doing this in a number of ways. They may point out that something the person has just said is totally incorrect and present data to support their assertion. They may put forward an unpleasant truth which makes the speaker and everyone around aware that what has just been said is at the least a gross exaggeration. When a pompous colleague's balloon is truly pricked and begins to deflate, it can result in two possible outcomes. First, the person descends to earth and sets aside his pomposity at least for some time, which is a good outcome for the team. But it can also lead to the person quickly filling up another balloon because such is the nature of people who love carrying inflated balloons.

Balloon on a Broken String

The award-winning author Haruki Murakami once said: 'I would be smiling and chatting away, and my mind would be floating around somewhere else, like a balloon with a broken string.' All of us who have endured boring, lengthy or meaningless meetings in office know exactly what he means. We remain physically present in our conference rooms during these meetings, but our mind is already like a balloon with a broken string, which has floated away into the vacation that is soon coming up, or delicious memories of the riotous party we enjoyed last weekend, or even the simple tasty fare that our lunchbox contains. The next time you are in such a meeting, look up for these loose balloons.

Balloons and Compliments

Let me conclude this essay with a beautiful quote about balloons that we can all consider adopting in our offices. Bernie Siegel, the American writer and surgeon, once said, 'Compliments are the helium that fills everyone's balloon. They elevate the person receiving them so that he or she can fly over life's troubles and land safely on the other side.' Conveying genuine compliments and appreciation to our colleagues in office is perhaps the best way of motivating them and making them fly higher than the best balloons.

Harish Bhat works with the Tata Group. He believes that every balloon which goes up must eventually come down.

7

Why Daydreaming Is a Good Thing

A few minutes spent drifting away can help one calm down, solve problems, increase productivity and nurture relationships.

How often have you looked out into nowhere and thought of pleasant things, or had your mind wander freely across various green pastures while in the midst of some important meeting, Zoom call or project work?

For most of our lives, we have been told to stop daydreaming and get back to work. The constant refrain we have heard, from many of our teachers and managers, is that daydreaming is a waste of time. Regardless, all of us continue to sit back and daydream every once in a while. And now it turns out that daydreaming is good for us.

Scientists think we spend as much as 45 per cent of our waking time daydreaming. And they believe that this helps us in many ways. Here's how.

Beating the Blues

All of us experience stress in our workplace and personal lives from time to time, and often this ends up exhausting us. Research shows daydreaming is an excellent method of getting away from stress-induced anxiety and exhaustion and restoring us to a state of happy equilibrium.

A Harvard University health blog authored by Srini Pillay, a psychiatrist and assistant professor at Harvard Medical School, points out that letting your mind wander away into nice things, far away from perceived threats, can lift you out of any negative spirals that you may have got into. And then, when you come back into your current reality, you can focus on your work much better because your mind is now feeling far more relaxed and positive. So, if you are experiencing anxiety, if a project is not going well or a meeting has been particularly difficult, try a little daydreaming so that you can return refreshed to tackle the tough issues.

Building Relationships

We often live and work far from our loved ones. Particularly at the height of the pandemic, many of us were unable to travel to meet family or friends frequently, and did not meet many of our colleagues in person for long bursts of time. Studies show that daydreaming about people who are special and important to you, as also about colleagues and office moments that fill you with positive energy, helps keep these relationships alive in our minds. For instance, sitting back and daydreaming about a really productive physical offsite meeting two years ago, where your team and you came up with a great product or sales idea, which was then followed by a celebration, helps you maintain a positive connect with those colleagues. Of course, this is no real substitute to meeting people in person, but it helps ensure that important relationships are kept alive through positive memories.

Solving Difficult Problems

Daydreaming also helps us solve challenging problems that we may be wrestling with. Often, we are so heavily immersed in these problems that our mind stops working after a while. Most of us face this mental block from time to time and when this happens, more of linear and logical thinking, however well-intentioned or intense, will just not help. A wandering mind, on the other hand, tends to use many different sections of the brain together, accessing the past knowledge and thoughts stored in diverse pockets of our minds, and weaving these together for a possible Eureka moment, where the solution we are desperately seeking suddenly becomes visible to us. I have found that saturating my mind with different aspects of the issue that requires resolution, and then engaging in some relaxed daydreaming a day or two later, can be a potent combination for problem solving.

Working towards a Goal

The American clinical psychologist Jerome L. Singer, who is, interestingly, regarded as the 'father of daydreaming', put forward the idea of 'positive-constructive daydreaming' and how it can help us in planning our future lives. When we daydream about a desirable future state that we would like to be in, we are able to freely ruminate on all the scenarios and steps that can possibly lead us to this goal. For instance, if you wish to become an accomplished marathon runner, then daydreaming about all the multiple things you can do from now until you accomplish your goal—what you will eat, how you will build muscle and stamina, the neighbourhood runs you will begin with, the training groups you would like to join and, finally, finishing the Mumbai or New York marathon in a burst of happiness—will help you constantly wire and adapt your mind to eventually achieve this success. Of course, for such constructive daydreaming, it is important that your goal should lie within the realms of possibility, however distant, and not veer off into some wild fantasy.

Sheer Pleasure

One of the best reasons to daydream is that this is truly a pleasurable activity. In our hectic lives, daydreaming provides a soft refuge to indulge in our most cherished thoughts. And, as all of us know, most pleasurable activities lift our mood and help us perform our tasks with renewed energy. Like a coffee break, a daydreaming break provides us a unique sense of happiness, whether we are peering at a laptop in our home office or gazing out at the clean sands and blue waters of a beach. It helps us pause the world, bring up our finest memories, reflect on our lives, imagine new things, all without any immediate pressure to perform. The best part is that each of us can daydream by ourselves, without any dependence on anyone else. Therefore, even the pandemic has not affected our ability to daydream every day, wherever we are. And we can then come back to our real lives feeling totally refreshed.

Daydreaming while walking alone or idly looking out of the window has helped me come up with many new ideas for marketing campaigns, books and articles.

8

Why Writing Makes Us Happier

*The daily practice of putting pen to paper will
make your day as well as life better.*

Ask professionals about writing, and you are likely to get diverse
responses. There are some, like me, who love the written word.
There are others who wish to write but never get around to it
because they have so many other things to do. And then there
are some who do not write because they either simply dislike
putting pen to paper or feel they have little to write about.

I think writing is for everyone. For, it has the power to make
us really happy. Whether you write books, articles, blogs, emails
or your own personal diary, here is an art form that is easy to
pursue and fulfilling.

Why does writing lead to happiness? Here are some
compelling reasons.

A Sharpener

We live with many thoughts and ideas in our mind. These could
be ideas for the next project in office, thoughts on a forthcoming

marketing campaign, say, or some reflections that a nice video on YouTube has triggered.

These thoughts are often initially fuzzy, and evolve either through deep thinking or after discussion with our colleagues. Either way, when you start writing to articulate these ideas and what they mean to you, you end up sharpening the thoughts themselves.

This happens because writing focuses our mind and compels us to be as clear and precise as possible. And, of course, when we are able to crystallise our thoughts in this fashion, we certainly feel happy.

A Lifter

I have found writing to be a great mood lifter, especially when I'm feeling down and out, or when work is particularly stressful.

Adam Grant, organizational psychologist at Wharton and a bestselling author, tells us that writing about our work and its impact makes us more productive and happy. This is particularly the case when we are caught in the midst of stressful, fast-paced work. Penning down the positive impact we have been able to create can give us a new boost of energy. Similarly, writing about what we wish to achieve in the future, even if these goals are still quite distant, makes us happy because it clearly outlines for us the dreams that we want to move towards. Our dreams give us hope and seeing them clearly articulated on paper make them even more real and tangible in our mind.

A Thank-You Note

There is considerable research to show that feelings of gratitude make us happy. Writing helps us express our gratitude in authentic and intimate ways—something that is sometimes difficult to do verbally.

For instance, writing a weekly diary, where we record all that we are grateful for, helps us see how much happiness, big or small, has come into our lives over the past seven days, notwithstanding a challenging environment such as the Covid-19 pandemic. Writing a small letter, email or even a WhatsApp message to convey genuine gratitude to a colleague, also makes us happy because we are adding a few smiles and some positivity to another person's life. We sometimes do not realize the enormous power of these small written gestures of gratitude. I have treasured some of these messages for years thereafter and so have many of my colleagues.

A Reminder

We come across so many interesting and relevant things each day. Sometimes a book or an article or even a WhatsApp forward throws up good ideas that we may wish to use. Often, we attend a lecture or webinar where a few compelling points are put forward. At other times, a wonderful idea may occur to us at a random moment, when we are commuting or daydreaming or even while taking a shower. These ideas often get waylaid in our over-crowded minds as we quickly move on to some other activity. With time, these thoughts may get lost altogether.

The best way of archiving ideas for future reference is to write them down. I have seen some colleagues carry a little notebook with them all the time for precisely this reason. You may or may not use these thoughts later but by writing them down, you can feel happy that you'll not lose them. It is quite likely that you may revisit some of these written ideas at a later date, to develop them further.

An Influencer

Many of us wish to contribute to our professional world by making a positive impact through our ideas and reflections.

The ability to influence thinking in our specific sphere of work or interest inevitably creates happiness in our mind, even fulfilment. Sometimes this is also important to our roles. Writing is perhaps the easiest way to develop such thought leadership.

Once you have penned down your thoughts and posted them on a public platform, they can travel far and wide. I write often on LinkedIn on my areas of interest. When a reader then comments on how my article has helped or inspired them, I feel motivated to contribute even more. This is a positive spiral of ideation, and writing is often the best starting point.

An Art

Finally, for many of us, writing also brings immense happiness because it is such a beautiful art form. Finding the right phrase, crafting a seamless flow of words, selecting the right metaphor, injecting a bit of humour, refining the prose, discarding jargon, and clearly and succinctly conveying a complex idea—these are all integral parts of the joy that writing brings.

You do not have to be a professional writer to experience these delights. As you keep writing, you will find that your love for the written word also evolves, and you will soon become a wordsmith in your own style.

I find that writing is also therapy for the mind as it often settles my thinking and gives me both space and peace.

9

A Beginner's Guide to Recovering from Meetings

Bad meetings can set back your day, unless you have strategies to recover from them.

A lot has been written about how we can make meetings in our workplaces more effective. Fewer and shorter meetings, clearer agendas, more focused discussions, no long-winded presentations—all these desirable actions are now well known. Happily, they are even being adopted by some wise managers. But at the end of the day, the harsh truth is that we still continue to constantly be in many bad meetings which leave us in a funk. And unless we find good, practical ways of quickly recovering from such useless sessions, our entire day goes for a toss.

Listen to what Joseph Allen, a professor of occupational and environmental health at the University of Utah, has to say. He says that when an employee sits through an ineffective meeting, their brain power is essentially being drained away. From experience, I can testify that this melting of the brain then leads to a sharp decline in productivity. This happens because the mind winds down to a standstill, frustrated and even numbed by the terrible meeting that has just concluded.

For all of us who have felt this mind-draining sensation after meetings, what we need is a toolkit for quick recovery. Here is a beginner's guide based not on detailed research but on total common sense.

Half an Hour of Personal Space

To unwind after a meeting and restore mental balance before you take up your next bit of work, you have to provide yourself at least half an hour of personal space. During this time, reflect a little on the meeting gone by, and then let it pass completely. If possible, think of some ridiculous things that were said during the meeting and smile, even if you have to occasionally laugh at yourself. Nothing is that serious, and laughter always helps. A long walk helps too. I know a colleague who promptly vanishes after each meeting, in a hurry, and I used to often wonder why he does this. Now I think I know.

A Safe and Comforting Place

When you leave a meeting that has been particularly threatening or confrontational, it helps to dump your papers on your desk, and go immediately to a place you find safe and comforting. This could be the office canteen or a close friend's desk or even a cafe down the road. Sit there for some time, even if you sit in complete silence. The important thing is to distance yourself physically, far away from the venue of the earlier hostilities. Slowly, the friendly vibes return, and you find your anger or helplessness melting away. That puts you in a better position to make the mental switch to your next task.

Digital Browsing

While I am not a fan of aimless digital browsing and socializing, I acknowledge that such mindless cyber-wandering often has a therapeutic effect on a disturbed mind. Therefore, I have no hesitation in recommending this practice to everyone trying to bounce back from a bad meeting. Pick up your mobile phone, browse your favourite shopping sites, WhatsApp a few random friends with lots of emojis thrown in, wander around your Facebook or Instagram. If you are particularly upset, try watching some inane Tik Tok videos. All this should work like magic. And if you are the gaming type, play a few favourite digital games. I am told that violent sort of games can even help dissipate your anger.

Like-Minded Colleagues

If you have had a bad meeting, it is likely that a few other participants, who are like-minded, have also suffered a similar fate. And, with experience, each of us knows who our like-minded colleagues are. So, it helps to have an informal catch-up with these colleagues post the meeting, just to compare notes. This helps build invaluable perspective on what really happened in the meeting, and why. Such conversations throw up interesting analyses of matters such as the undercurrents that ran through the meeting, or the unbearable incompetence of a few individuals who dominated the discussions. And there's nothing like a conversation between friends to help you relax, and prepare for your next task ahead.

No More Useless Meetings

If you have just come out of a bad meeting, a good recovery strategy is to resolve not to attend any more poorly conducted or ineffective meetings. Make a note of the kind of meetings that put you off completely, or where nothing of value emerges, or sessions where you have little to contribute. And then tell yourself that you will not participate in any of this specific sort of meetings in the future unless you are compelled to. Then go ahead, and say a firm 'No' to such meeting requests. That decision alone will lift a big weight off your shoulders and you can move forward with a spring in your step to some other work that gives you real joy.

Great Coffee and Tea

For many of us, the best and easiest way to recover from a bad meeting is a hot cup of coffee or tea. There is inexhaustible warmth, happiness and magic in these wonderful beverages. Your weary body and mind will perk up right away as you sip your cappuccino or green tea and contemplate pleasant things which are far more important than the just-concluded frustrating session. Keep a nice, happy-looking mug on your table for these restorative coffee breaks. And, if possible, get yourself some great tasting single-origin coffee that takes you deep into the sort of places that nourish your soul.

10

Dump the Slides; Add Power to Your Point

Long PowerPoint presentations are a waste of time and energy. Here are some interesting alternatives.

Many of us have silently suffered long meetings where presentations go on and on. Slick PowerPoint slides, lots of them, with amazing visuals and mind-altering fonts, come at you from articulate presenters determined to impress. But at the end of the meeting, you are often left asking yourself: What have all these presentations really accomplished?

A study published in the *Harvard Business Review* concluded that presentations work well only when a meeting is about communicating an already formed idea, or when the objective is to inform, persuade or entertain an audience, without requiring real-time feedback from participants. On the other hand, when you call for a meeting to develop or flesh out an idea, get inputs or consensus on the way forward, or build a personal relationship with the participants, then the approach which works the best is to encourage conversations rather than schedule presentations. In other words, for these sorts of meetings, we should prioritize conversations over presentations (COP). Let's call this the good-COP approach. Here is a primer on good-COP meetings, with some ideas on how you can make them happen.

Ban PowerPoint

A radical good-COP approach to meetings is to ban PowerPoint presentations altogether. Jeff Bezos has famously done this at Amazon. There, everyone sits silently for the first several minutes of the meeting, reading a six-page narrative memo that sets the context for the meeting, including the subject at hand. The rest of the meeting is then a conversation on the subject, with key decisions being summarized at the end.

Bezos believes the narrative structure of a good memo forces better thought and understanding of the issue, compared to bullet points on presentations. After all, human brains are configured for narratives and storytelling, not for a stream of bullet points. The silent reading period ahead of the conversation also ensures that no one bluffs their way into meetings, without having done the required preparation. We know some of those people, don't we?

Five-Slide Rule

If you don't wish to be as radical as Amazon, then a good-COP way is to insist on a very slim presentation at any meeting, not more than five slides in length. There is no subject on this planet whose essence cannot be put forward in five good slides, though it takes a lot of thoughtfulness to ensure such brevity. A more detailed document can be circulated ahead of the meeting, for pre-reading. However, you run a real risk here because there is no research evidence yet on how many participants actually read a pre-read document.

The five-slide rule often gets diluted by presenters slipping in a sixth or seventh slide, and then, there is no stopping the deluge. So, if you pursue this path, take a simple mathematical approach to numbers, that is, five equals five. It is a fine number—easy to keep count on our fingertips. Also, the five slides should be carefully crafted to provoke meaningful conversation.

Use Flipcharts

There exists in Switzerland an organization called the Anti-PowerPoint Party. This is a political party dedicated to decreasing the use of PowerPoint and other presentation software, because they believe that fancy presentations cause significant economic damage by wasting lots of effort and time. This party strongly advocates the use of flipcharts in meetings instead of presentations.

Flipcharts (or even whiteboards) are an amazing alternative to presentations, to trigger good conversation at meetings. They help you co-create the narrative along with participants, a far more engaging process than a one-sided projection of slides. Flipcharts evolve and flow with the conversation in a meeting. Participants can engage with the presenter to make the required changes on the charts, no energy is dissipated on wasteful hi-tech razzmatazz, the message gets through more interactively and eventually the required actions are co-created by everyone in the room. So, try a flipchart solution next time, and see how well it works for your team.

Roundtable Conversations

Some of the most productive good-COP meetings I have attended have been round-table conversations, anchored by a good leader, who gets things moving. Without presentations or flipcharts, the chairperson of the meeting highlights the objectives and agenda and guides the conversation skilfully around all relevant points. Sometimes, he or she delivers his or her opening remarks on the subject, from simple handwritten notes that capture the essence of the subject. The chairperson also creates deliberate pauses for discussion, along the way.

This sort of good-COP meeting requires the chairperson to have clarity, an open mind, and excellent listening, conversational and navigation skills. In addition, a sense of humour helps immensely. Such meetings work best if members around the roundtable know each other well enough to engage in free-flowing, candid conversation.

So, be a good COP and dump that bulky presentation. Your move will transfer all power to the points you really wish to discuss at the meeting, and you will also, happily, bring an end to much silent suffering.

I often wonder what's happened to all those simple acetate slides we used on overhead projectors so many years ago. Sometimes the power of simplicity trumps the march of technology.

11

New Laws of the Digital Workplace

Six not-so-serious axioms which every office worker in today's digital era needs to know.

Newton's laws are a familiar memory from school—the most famous being that for every action there is an equal and opposite reaction. Equally, and painfully familiar, is Parkinson's law: work expands so as to fill the time available for its completion. No wonder things always get done at the last minute.

But in today's workplace, where digital devices and platforms rule our lives, it is important to establish new laws: the laws of the digital workplace. Since no famous business guru has yet undertaken this endeavour, I am stepping in to fill this new-age gap. Here, therefore, I bring you a compilation of the digital laws which every office worker should be aware of.

Mobile Distance Axiom

This axiom states that the distance between a person and his or her mobile phone is inversely correlated to the amount of productive work that gets done.

In other words, if your mobile phone is close to you, and if you are a normal human being who is prone to temptation, then tough luck. You will end up checking your WhatsApp, social media and emails on your phone so often that it becomes difficult to have a focused discussion or get creative work done. A corollary to this axiom is that wise executives keep their mobile phones far away during important meetings.

Fifty-Per-Cent Rule

This rule simply states that on a normal day, at least 50 per cent of all people who attend a meeting will be busy reading or writing messages on their laptops, tablets or mobile phones. Therefore, it is unlikely they are paying serious attention to the proceedings of the meeting. At large, irrelevant conferences, where every participant is generally anonymous in the midst of hundreds of people, this percentage can creep close to 100.

The corollary to this rule is that the chairperson of any important meeting would do well to request all participants to turn off all their digital devices, or keep them out of sight, until the meeting concludes.

Law of Infinite Messages

The Law of Infinite Messages reveals a great digital truth. The number of emails and messages that reach you every day are too many to count, and there is no end to how quickly they pop into your inbox, messaging apps or social media timelines. Therefore, it is futile to try to read or respond to each, and any such well-intended effort is doomed to failure.

An outcome of this law is that good managers develop the fine art of quickly identifying all the digital noise that they need to totally ignore and simultaneously pick out the very few messages that they must pay attention to.

Group Disruption Theorem

This postulates that each manager is part of at least one digital group that threatens to disrupt his or her life every day. This could be a work group on some shared digital platform, a WhatsApp group of college batchmates, a Google group of residents of your apartment building or an ad-hoc group on LinkedIn to which you have recently been added for reasons you are still trying to fathom. At least one of these digital groups will post one or more provocative messages during the day, which will seize and disrupt your mind space completely.

For instance, your apartment's Google group could suddenly post a message informing you that there has been a serious water leakage in all kitchens. That's enough to disrupt everything else for the moment, including the strategy document on which you have been trying to work.

Of course, no strategy is worthwhile if the kitchen is getting flooded. Digital gurus are still hunting for the corollary to this theorem.

Day and Night Rule

This rule states that digital devices are uniformly active during the day and night, as they don't need any rest. Unfortunately, we humans are creatures of tired muscles and fraying nerves so we need good, deep sleep—eight hours a day, albeit a distant goal for many of us, should be the norm. All this creates a situation where the same digital devices that are our inseparable friends during the day try to intrude into our nights.

There is only one good solution. Switch off your digital devices at a specified time each night, ideally at least half an hour before you get to bed. Then sleep well, as far as possible from the digital world.

The Sunrise Postulate

Your agenda for the day is set first and foremost by your digital behaviour as soon as you wake up.

If you check your digital devices first thing in the morning and begin responding to the various messages received during the night, that is exactly the way your day will flow. On the other hand, if you ignore all this digital noise at sunrise and first set your priorities for the day, then you have far greater control over what you will achieve over the next several hours. If you are not the type that wakes up around sunrise or if you do not sleep at all, then you are beyond this postulate.

I am a strong proponent of Occam's digital razor, a new-age version of an age-old philosophy, which states that to live and work happily, you should minimize the number of digital devices you use. Zero is brilliant but rare, one is fine, two is tolerable, three is a noisy crowd and four is a mad stampede.

12

Your Office Companion Spills the Beans

That cup sitting on your desk can give a lot of clues about who you are.

Tea and coffee are our constant companions in office. Our tastes may vary between cappuccino, espresso, masala chai and green tea but most of us drink, on an average, three to five hot beverages each day at work. This also means that the cups in which we drink tea and coffee are our steadfast companions too.

No wonder these cups and mugs have become interesting statements of personal style, and even integral elements of office culture. Gone are the days when you drank your coffee or tea in a nondescript white cup and saucer. Look around your office, and one of the most colourful and diverse areas will be the pantry cupboard where the mugs and cups are stored.

Taste in mugs and cups speak volumes about the executive who drinks from them. Here is a cup primer that walks us through some interesting varieties you can choose from.

Porcelain China Cups

In some of the most distinguished offices, you are still served tea and coffee in the time-honoured tradition—in delicate porcelain china cups, tastefully designed, and often with a little touch of gold at the rim. These are executives who believe in the power of tradition and, in all likelihood, they will also offer you sponge cake or Marie biscuits with your beverage at evening teatime. A word of caution. Porcelain is delicate, so be careful with these cups and also with your conversation in these hallowed halls. In such wood-panelled offices, you are advised to keep your conversation formal, sip your tea elegantly and leave as soon as you have accomplished what you came for.

Conversation Starters

These mugs are printed with colourful photographs of the executive, and perhaps his or her spouse or partner or children or even pet dogs. The idea here is to bring the family right into the workplace. When you meet a colleague drinking out of such a family mug, you should occasionally ask him or her about the family, and particularly about the pets. People with pets love speaking about them and this can be a very useful icebreaker before you get on to essential business discussion.

Alma Mater Mugs

Increasingly, many executives use coffee mugs emblazoned with the logos of universities. Such mugs tend to primarily reflect nostalgia for the alma mater. Very importantly, they give you valuable insights into the executive—for instance, if he has a mug which says Indian Institute of Technology (IIT) or Indian Institute of Management (IIM) or some such similar name, he will, in all likelihood, be a left-brained, numbers guy. Sometimes you may see people carrying around mugs with globally famous college names such as Harvard or Cambridge. This does not necessarily mean that they have studied there; it could reflect just an aspiration or a deep need for badge value. In such cases, do your own research before jumping to any conclusions.

Holiday Postcards

When you see colleagues drinking tea from mugs that feature a beach in the Bahamas or a chateau in France, you must speak to them about their holiday. Here is an executive who is very proud of his vacation, and his cup is virtually a picture postcard that he is putting in front of you. He will talk fondly about time he spent walking the cobbled streets of Paris or drinking tankards of beer at Oktoberfest in Munich. You can then respond by speaking about your own holiday in Cambodia or Japan. There cannot be a better way of bonding between stressed-out office colleagues who are taking a well-deserved tea break before rushing to their next long and tiring meeting.

Latte Lifestyle

A growing segment of executives loves to be seen with disposable cups that feature famous brands of coffee or tea. The green or red logo on the cup is the important thing here. This is a statement of a cool lifestyle, and also a signal that the person is (or wishes to be) a connoisseur of the hallowed beverage, that he or she seeks only the best and finest. You can spend hours discussing with him or her the relative merits of a latte, cappuccino, espresso, Darjeeling first flush tea or Mao Feng green tea. The cup also provides good insights into where exactly you can invite the person for your next meeting.

Dash of Humour

For managers who wish to inject a bit of humour into their workplace, the surface area of mugs is a good place to turn to. Mugs carry humour lightly and convey the message that you are not a serious, stuck-up guy. There is, of course, a wide variety of messages to choose from, so you will never run out of options. Some popular one-liners I have seen on mugs are: 'Compliance is my life', 'I love the Human Resources Department', 'The Devil made me do it', 'I had my patience tested, I'm negative'. The real trick here is to have a message that you believe in and is humorous at the same time. That makes for a mug that you will be happy to carry and use all day.

I loved drinking from my college mug, which featured the clock tower at BITS Pilani, until it broke a few years ago.

13

Do You Ask Questions That Really Matter?

Managers who ask the right questions are better informed and more likeable.

Conversations between colleagues are an integral part of our offices, and they define much of our workplace experience. In India, as in some other parts of the world, we love speaking. But there is one key aspect of conversations that many of us have not consciously focused on—the art of asking questions. Are we asking the right questions, in the appropriate manner, at the right time?

I attempt to answer this important question here, based on research that has been carried out at Harvard University, as well as my own experience and that of some of my colleagues. If you reflect carefully on discussions in your own office, you are likely to conclude that not enough of the right kind of questions are being asked. Some questions are posed rhetorically; quite often questions are asked merely to impress others, and then there are lots of lazy questions which do not delve deep enough. Such questions often do more harm than good, and are also a recurring source of irritation. On the other hand, you will find that people who ask the right questions regularly, in a conducive manner, add a lot of value and are generally respected.

So here are some home truths about asking questions.

First, Ask Questions

If you are seeking information, it is important that you ask questions. How else will you get the answers you require? In most conversations, people spend an inordinate proportion of time speaking about themselves, what they have achieved, their own feelings and experiences, rather than asking questions about others. Such loquacious behaviour may occasionally help to impress the other person, but very soon most others are likely to lose interest, unless you are bringing many fresh ideas to the table. On the other hand, if you ask relevant questions, there is a good probability that you will be rewarded with new learning. And, in addition, people around you will know that you are curious, and are engaged in what they are saying. As a result, you are likely to be naturally included in the flow of the conversation.

Avoid Useless Questions

Many of us arrive at work each morning and dutifully ask each other: 'How are you?' There is growing evidence that this is a useless question, because the answer is mostly predictable: 'I am doing fine, and how are you?' Even if the other person is in the throes of a terrible crisis in his life, he is unlikely to open up to you in response to this rhetorical question. Why? Because, this is just an exchange of pleasantries. The questioner is not really bothered about the response to his question, and the person answering does not care to be frank either. On the other hand, if you were to ask your early morning colleague pleasant and easily answerable questions such as: 'What are you planning to do this weekend?' or 'What food are you planning to treat yourself to this week?', you may get interesting responses which may actually start off a real, personal conversation.

Power of Follow-Up Questions

Some of the most powerful queries are follow-up questions. When you listen to a person speaking and then ask questions that follow up on the same topic, you are likely to get very good answers. This happens because, in the first place, the speaker possesses some knowledge of that subject, and second, because the speaker has now sensed your interest in what she has said. Therefore she is willing to explore your question, and this quickly pushes the conversation beyond the superficial. A series of follow-up questions and answers is perhaps the best method of ensuring that a discussion becomes a meaningful and fulfilling conversation.

There is an added benefit to asking follow-up questions. In a research paper published in the *Journal of Personality and Social Psychology*, titled 'It Doesn't Hurt to Ask: Question-Asking Increases Liking', five professors from Harvard University point out that people who ask follow-up questions tend to be better liked by their conversation partners because they are seen as being higher in responsiveness. Now, that's an added bonus—

you get your answers, and you also end up being better liked by your colleagues!

Crafting Great Questions

To trigger great conversations, figure out what are the most interesting and insightful questions that you can ask your colleagues, in the context of the meeting you are engaged in. For instance, if you are at a sales review, ask the sales team what were the top three things they did that helped them achieve the sales results they are presenting at the meeting, rather than merely congratulating them on the results. Ask questions such as: what has been the most exciting thing you learnt last month about our customers? What challenges did you face this season and how did you try to address these? Can you share one nice story from our retail stores that you are really proud of? What is the most important thing I should know about the new members of your team? In other words, go beyond the cursory small talk or the usual routine, and ask questions that open doors for people to share their real experiences and perspectives with you. If your questions touch the areas that matter, watch how the discussion quickly moves into deep and constructive conversation.

Finally, never ever stop yourself from asking a question just because you are worried that it may be perceived as idiotic or may portray you as incompetent. Often, the unexpectedly simple questions unearth the most insightful answers.

My aspiration is to ask one great question each day. The big question is: 'When will I begin doing this?'

14

Make February Your New January

After grand visioning in January, get down to achieving your goals in February.

February is a sobering month for all office workers. To begin with, it has only twenty-eight days, so it offers us that much less time to meet the month's sales targets and other important goals. Then, of course, the euphoria of a champagne-fuelled new year has faded completely by then, and many grand resolutions are, unfortunately, burning out. Studies show that by the beginning of February, 80 per cent of all New Year resolutions have been quietly buried.

This is precisely why managers should consider making February the start of a fresh new year, for resolutions that we really wish to achieve. Here is a month where realism has dawned and we are grappling with what we can actually achieve, rather than a fantastic wish list. Even the name February is derived from Februa, the ancient Roman feast which was celebrated to re-establish focus on righteous living. It is the right time, therefore, to focus on your essential resolutions for the year ahead. You can reflect on the month gone by, what has worked and what has not, and also define the first steps that are essential for any grand plan. To use corporate jargon, if January has been a month of grand visioning, February is the month when we can commence brass tacks execution.

Here are some suggestions which may encourage you to pursue this February approach.

Power of Three

First and foremost, cut down your well-intentioned but overly ambitious New Year's list to define not more than three essential resolutions for the year. More than three is a bad idea unless you possess some superhuman managerial and human skills. There is something about the power of three which energizes us—three is a stretch, yet within our grasp. It is always three medals for winners, the trinity in religion, three musketeers in literature, three idiots in the movies. I have found that three is a good number to begin with.

Second, list out your three resolutions in very simple terms, along with an essential first step that you need to take to get them going. Here are three examples that are relevant to office workers.

Fitness and Health

Most executives I know have a fitness and health resolution for the new year. This could include grand objectives such as wishing to run the marathon or developing six-pack abs. But remember that we are office workers who have to be at our workplaces every day, and we also have bodies that are at varying sagging levels of fitness after endless meetings, eating and travel. So, put down simple objectives to begin with—such as some sort of physical exercise five times a week, ranging from gym workouts to walking up the stairs in office. Based on your office schedules, define whether you will complete this activity in the mornings or after work. Most importantly, commit yourself to first steps to make this happen. For instance, this could be a commitment to the next twenty-one sessions of physical exercise. Empirical evidence shows that most things become a habit if you persist for twenty-one days. February, with twenty-eight days, is a good month to complete these twenty-one sessions. Don't drop your grand goal of running a marathon, that's a cool thing to do, but make it subordinate to these immediate steps.

Work-Life Balance

Few things are more elusive than the holy grail of work-life balance in the lives of working professionals. We veer between periods of severe imbalance and constant juggling, even as we try to desperately understand what constitutes balance. Grand terms such as work-life harmony and holistic living, used liberally by iconic global leaders, muddy these waters further. So, to achieve some clarity, define what balance means specifically for you, for the year ahead. It could simply mean the ability and bandwidth to spend two quality hours every day with your spouse and child and being fully available to your family for any emergency. It could also mean pursuing one hobby that you are passionate about, in addition to excelling at your workplace. Or it could mean two happy vacations during the year.

Perhaps a first step you can define is that you will not stay late in office any day, unless there is a genuine crisis, and that you will have dinner with your family every night. Try the twenty-one-day commitment here too.

Beating Digital Addiction

One of my goals for the year ahead is to beat digital addiction, with its constant distractions and frequent interruptions. I suspect this may be true for many executives, because we surely don't want our mobile phones to rule our lives, though the truth is that they are constantly trying to enslave us. Yet, none of us can be digital recluses in today's connected world.

Here again, a good and practical resolution could be to use digital devices only within a certain time during the day. Never use them during meetings and never late at night, which I have, with great hope, defined as 10 p.m. for myself. A first step could be to leave your phone far from your seat at a meeting, and even further from your bed at night.

These are only illustrations, and the three resolutions you want to pursue could be quite different. Pin up your three February New Year's resolutions, with first steps highlighted in green, on your softboard in front of you, so that you can see them clearly each day. Request your boss to include these resolutions in your statement of annual goals, because they will ultimately also make you a better professional. In most organizations, goal-setting occurs during March, for the financial year that begins in April—all the more reason to make February the start of a wonderful new march towards your goals.

I would earnestly like to practise what I have preached in this piece, and am currently grappling with bringing down my eight unworkable resolutions to three.

15

Listening: A Vital Managerial Skill

The deepest listening often occurs in total silence, and with an open mind.

We don't listen well enough. Many managers, like me, speak well, read well, make grand presentations, try hard to lead from the front and also attempt a host of other good official deeds, for which we deserve due commendation. But sadly, we are poor listeners. Often, we may hear, but we don't listen.

This is despite the fact that for most professions, over 75 per cent of the work is based on listening to others. Imagine a marketer not listening to his customers, or an HR professional not listening to young managers, or a leader not listening to her team members. So, most people will agree that listening is a powerful and essential managerial skill. Unfortunately, it is not a skill that receives adequate focus, either in business schools or in organizations. Here are some simple suggestions on how we can listen better.

Keep Quiet

We love hearing the sound of our own voice, so we don't keep our mouths shut as much as we should. But to listen carefully to someone else, you have to shut up. The deepest listening often occurs in total silence, where what you are hearing can be absorbed by your mind, without having to contend with the clutter of extraneous noise. I find that when I am tempted to speak out of turn, which is quite often, putting my finger on my lips is a good way to shut up. My primary school teacher taught me that many decades ago.

Open Your Mind

To listen, you need an open mind. Often, when we hear something that goes against the grain of our existing belief, we tend not to listen any more, simply because we don't wish to hear that we are wrong. Defences build up immediately in our mind, and then we are done. On the other hand, most new ideas emerge from something that is not aligned to existing knowledge. So, the best way to listen is to keep your ears wide open for negative evidence—evidence that says you are wrong—and pay particular attention to why the speaker thinks that way. Don't begin the process of evaluation until you have heard him/her out fully. An open mind does not guarantee you true enlightenment, but it certainly helps.

Put Away Your Phone

Opening your mind during a meeting does not help if you have simultaneously also opened your mobile phone or laptop. When you are listening to your colleague speak, put away your digital devices and watch the positive energy flow. WhatsApp, social media and email tend to insulate you from the outside world. On the other hand, two or more people, face to face, discussing a topic without any digital distraction threatening to raise its head, makes for the best listening platform. A colleague of mine always places his bright red mobile phone right at the other corner of the room before he sits at any important meeting. He says it helps to keep temptation far away.

Forget the Food

Our listening ability is, unfortunately, inversely correlated with our hunger and our abiding interest in food. As mealtime approaches, a few participants begin actively daydreaming about what could be on the menu for lunch or dinner, which is a recipe for delicious distraction from the subject at hand. But we do need to reckon with the pangs of hunger, which are totally real, and yet find ways of remaining unmoved. I find that carrying a small hardboiled sweet in my pocket is a very helpful device. When hunger strikes, I pop the sweet into my mouth and roll it around my tongue, which helps me to continue listening intently until the meal break.

Wait, Then Ask

Once you have listened well, and there is a natural pause in the speaker's flow of conversation, it is a good idea to ask questions that help bring clarity to your own thinking. Don't hesitate to do this, because productive listening requires clarity. Asking a colleague who has come to speak to you to clarify exactly what he means or really needs from you reassures both of you that you are thinking in the same direction. But unless there is some compelling urgency such as an intergalactic corporate shutdown within the next five minutes, don't interrupt a speaker—that will spoil your own voyage of listening and also irritate everyone else.

Listen with All Senses

If you wish to listen well, pay attention to non-verbal cues as they are important to what is being said. The best listeners carefully observe the speaker's face and body language to understand what is really being meant, including the subtext. This is quite an art, because you must know what to observe and it is never good to be caught staring. How something is said, and what is left unsaid, is equally important. Once, I heard and saw one of my team members become totally and instantly energized while speaking about a certain topic in consumer behaviour, and I knew instantly where his heart and mind lay. It helped me assign him to exactly the right project when the opportunity came up, and he is now a star performer there.

Leave Useless Meetings

There is no documented research yet on the number of totally useless meetings that each of us attends and listens in to. But the results of such a study would be quite revealing, I am sure. Once we are in a meeting or conversation, we generally tend to stay there and listen listlessly until the session has concluded—even if we discover the subject to be boring or quite irrelevant to our needs. Perhaps we do this as a matter of courtesy, or maybe because our boss is around, or even out of sheer inertia. Nothing could be more damaging. It is always preferable to stop listening and politely excuse yourself, which is acceptable in many such sessions, though not always.

In addition to all the above, I would also like to create the space and time to listen more often to myself.

16

Pandemic Habits We Should Stick To

Being kind to oneself and other good behaviours that can make us happier and more effective.

With the worst of Covid-19 behind us now, we can hope and pray for normalcy, joy and happiness. We hope this terrible pandemic, which sapped us over the past two years, just goes away and never returns.

While we look forward to these big positive changes, we can't overlook the fact that there are also many good habits the pandemic has inculcated in us. Many of these behaviours have made us better human beings, and more effective, efficient and self-aware professionals.

Even as the year ends, we should reflect on these habits, because they are worth carrying forward into the new year. Here's a look at some of them and why they are worth keeping.

Be Kind to Yourself Too

We have endured multiple lockdowns, illnesses in the family, layoffs, isolation from our colleagues and friends. Many of us have grappled with how best to live through this difficult, somewhat surreal time. One lesson that has emerged from this trying period is the need to be kind to oneself.

This is perhaps the best antidote to combating stress.

While many of us like to be productive every day and deal successfully with all the challenges that life throws at us, the stresses of the pandemic have taught us that it is equally important not to hold ourselves to superhuman standards all the time. We can be kind to ourselves in many simple ways. For instance, by eating and sleeping well, enjoying simple pleasures such as a delicious meal or a nice walk every day, or taking a few minutes to meditate. I hope to take this learning forward, for sure.

Check Your Tone

Every time I have called a colleague or friend during the height of the pandemic, particularly people I was not in regular touch with, I often thought to myself: do I really know what is going on in their lives during this difficult time? I try to assess this during the first few minutes of the conversation, before getting down to brass tacks. The tone of my emails has become distinctly gentler, when I know the person on the other end has gone through a rough patch.

The pain of the second wave of Covid-19 reinforced in my mind the need for empathy, consciously putting ourselves in others' shoes as we interact with them. This is a good habit to cultivate in the future too because it makes us better human beings. In an increasingly divisive world, it will also make us a better society.

A To-Do List Always Matters

In the past, I have generally found it difficult to say no to requests from colleagues or friends. All with good intent, but this typically results in my to-do list overflowing at the brim. The year 2021 taught me the need to ruthlessly prioritize things, given the multiple demands the pandemic, as well as a bout of illness earlier in the year, brought into my life.

I now make only those commitments that my bandwidth and health permit me to take up, while ensuring that I leave some time for myself. And I do my best to ensure that I deliver on all these commitments to standards that I can be proud of. I think this has made me far more effective, as I give each task the mind-space which it deserves.

What's more, prioritization has also brought better balance into my life. Saying no to less important meetings and matters is certainly a habit worth taking forward.

Stay Creative

So many people I know have cultivated beautiful creative habits since the start of the pandemic. My wife has taken to active terrace gardening, and revels in it alongside her day job as a data scientist. A colleague has become an avid painter. A friend has begun making and selling dolls for charity. Two of my acquaintances at the workplace have published books of poetry.

Many of us have engaged in these creative pursuits to combat the stress and the bleak news of the pandemic.

During the year gone by, creativity has helped liberate our minds from the confines of the coronavirus. In the days ahead, these creative pursuits are certainly worth their weight in gold, because they help rejuvenate ourselves in so many wonderful ways.

The Power of Resilience

The ups and downs of 2021 have enabled an important self-discovery: we can be even more resilient that we ever imagined. Many people have lost loved ones to Covid-19. Loneliness has been a big issue, mainly for senior citizens. Layoffs have affected workers, particularly in some industry sectors. So many local businesses, including small- and medium-scale entrepreneurs, have faced tough market conditions. Lots of anticipated travel has been put on hold because of entry and quarantine restrictions.

Yet so many of us have bounced back each time, emerging from our tunnels with vigour and energy, determined to take life by its horns and move forward. We have begun living life with as much normalcy as we can, taking various pandemic-triggered undulations in our stride. Resilience is a wonderful thing; it sustains hope and makes life worth living. It will stand us in good stead in the New Year, too.

Wash Your Hands

And finally, let us not forget a simple, healthy habit that is worthwhile carrying forward. This pandemic has taught us how to wash our hands well and often enough.

This habit is admittedly not in the same league as the behaviours listed above, but it is perhaps far more important than any of them, given that it can stave off illness and save lives.

Here's hoping that we continue to wash our hands equally well going forward, even after the pandemic has hopefully gone away.

One good habit I picked up during the pandemic is yoga. I recommend this to everyone.

17

Tune into the Blues to Work Smart

Here are some ways to use the colour of 2020 and create a sharp blueprint for yourself.

Blue was declared the official colour of 2020, but it is actually a colour that is relevant to every year. The American Pantone Colour Institute, which made this announcement based on their trend forecast, said that blue is evocative of the vast and infinite skies, and that the colour is associated with communication, introspection, clarity and trust. There is evidence that blue aids in concentration and also challenges us to think more deeply.

Here are some interesting ways in which each of us can leverage the colour blue in the year ahead.

Make a Sharp Blueprint

One of the best ways to ensure a fulfilling year is to make a sharp blueprint for yourself. Blue should be the colour of this print precisely because it brings clarity to what you do.

A sharp blueprint needs just three big objectives. Don't clutter it with lists of ten or twenty objectives because that will diffuse the blue. The blueprint could include professional objectives (for example, deliver on the big e-commerce marketing project for my team), learning objectives (build a new digital coding skill for myself) and personal objectives (enjoy at least two vacations with my partner this year, preferably in Goa and Greece).

In fact, a good blueprint should contain objectives on all these three fronts.

Do Some Extra Thinking

Most managers, including this author, are generally addicted to action. That's what gets our adrenaline going. As a result, we leave little time for thinking. Change this.

Make this the year of blue-sky thinking for yourself, in at least a couple of areas at work that are more important to you.

Blue-sky thinking is exactly what it means: painting a picture of all new possibilities for your business against a clear blue sky, which has nothing at all to cloud your vision.

For instance, if you are working at a startup focused on getting people to eat healthy nuts, get your team together at least once a week to figure out hundreds of new ways to get people to use almonds, peanuts or walnuts for snacking, in lunch boxes, in spontaneous recipes and even in carefully curated fine dining. Simply, make time for blue-sky thinking every week.

Hit the Music

Work hard and smart during the year, but also take time out to listen to the blues. Blues music typically includes notes that charm your heart and rhythms that drive your worries away and lift your soul. That's why jazz relaxes and calms us down, which is essential in our fast-paced lives.

Each of us needs a passion outside work that will relax and rejuvenate us. Your own version of 'listening to the blues' may be to trek under a blue sky each month, or read by a blue seaside, or wear your blue sneakers and head out for a nice run each weekend.

The nice thing is, you can find your blues in any colour; it can be walking in a garden or dancing to peppy Bollywood songs.

Pick your passion, make some time for it each week and call it your blues. Your passion has the potential to transform your life.

Cut the Lights

The blue lights of our digital devices play havoc with our lives. They are addictive, they distract us and impinge on our sleep. Here is a 'blue' that you can think of toning down.

Our mobile phones are a vital need, of course, but we can decide to turn them off at a predetermined time each evening (for me, it is 10 p.m.), well before we go to bed.

We can resolve never to bring the blue digital lights to our family dining tables this year, so that we make more time to have real conversations with our loved ones over dinner.

We can determine to keep the blue light of our digital devices far away from us when we are in important meetings or discussions, where our attention has to be on the speaker and what she is saying, rather than on WhatsApp or emails that gate-crash their way into our dopamine-seeking minds.

If you cut the blue lights, you are creating the right environment to concentrate and communicate.

Good Versus Bad

Not all blues are good. To enjoy the year ahead, resolve to banish the morning blues. Also, there will be many ups and downs in our teams, and many things will not happen as we want them to because that's the nature of our workplaces as well as life. But that's no reason to yield to Monday morning blues or to the blues of disappointment.

The best way to banish all workplace blues is to be resilient, to enjoy the voyage as much as the result, to celebrate victories big or small and to relish everything we are doing.

What's more, if we remember to be always grateful for all the good things that have come our way, that will help keep the blues away as well.

Two methods I use to banish the blues are: read a nice book or relish a delicious cup of coffee.

18

Finding Hotspots for Ideas

There is plenty of room in our offices for ideation and creativity, if you can find the right places.

Every organization and team is constantly on the lookout for new ideas. We need ideas to power growth, delight customers, attract and retain talent, reduce costs and more. But formal conference rooms, where executives meet most often, are not always the best places to trigger ideas. They tend to be stiff and hierarchical, and attempts at ideation are frequently waylaid by a rigid agenda, or even by just poor placement of seats.

For ideation, teams tend to opt for off-sites, but despite our best efforts, we cannot keep going to exotic places all the time, for many good reasons, including cost and convenience. What this means is that we must necessarily look for spaces within our offices that can nurture the search for new ideas on a regular basis.

The good news is our offices hold many hotspots for ideas. The better news is, these spaces are all accessible to us, if we make the effort. Here is a primer on office hotspots you can use every time you want to think creatively.

Where Light Shines

Rooms that have lots of natural ventilation and daylight tend to serve as excellent spaces for ideation. The reason appears to be simple—a natural backdrop, adequate oxygen for our brains, and an immediate environment that supports our overall health and well-being helps our creative thinking process. That's why some green plants in the room also tend to help.

So, the next time your team wants to brainstorm, choose a room which is well-ventilated and throw open the blinds to let the daylight in. Then, watch the ideas flow.

Art Counts, Always

You can create spaces that inspire ideas by adding interesting articles, quotations, paintings and even a wall for scribbling.

Psychogeography, an interesting science, studies the effect of a geographic location on the emotions and behaviours of individuals. If we are seeking a creative space, psychogeography urges us to seek environments that inspire us, help us drop our inhibitions, and experience moments of intellect and imagination. An unusual sculpture that holds our attention, a picture that helps us relax, an object that helps our minds drift without getting lost—all these push us to think better and creatively.

Break It Up

Coffee and tea breaks in your office canteen or café are a wonderful way to trigger ideas.

Studies have shown that an active break in the middle of a busy day helps the brain to process information in a relaxed way, which can often lead to new insights. In addition, I think there is something special about coffee and tea that stokes our imagination.

That is why ideas for so many new books and films are conceived in a café, over a stimulating cuppa. So, when your mind is saturated with discussion and desperately needs to make that breakthrough, heading to a café or canteen may be the best thing to do.

Thinking Corners

We need to develop our own favourite office corners for reflection and creative thinking. Each office has its own nooks and happy, quiet places. For you, this could be a cosy chair in the small office library. Or it may be a landing on the staircase, overlooking the street. Or a chair at the reception area, where you remain within the buzz of conversation but undisturbed otherwise. Sometimes your own workspace can become a thinking corner, with an audio headset to help you concentrate. If you are fortunate to be in a large corporate campus, then under a nice tree is a good place too.

'Go Take a Walk'

One of the best methods of idea generation in offices is to walk and talk with a couple of members of your team. In an interesting research paper titled 'Give Your Ideas Some Legs: The Positive Effect of Walking on Creative Thinking', professors Marily Oppezzo and Daniel L. Schwartz of Stanford University highlight the positive effect that walking has on creative thinking. Why does this happen? Perhaps because walking relaxes suppression of memories and brings forth ideas from within your mind.

The philosopher Friedrich Nietzsche once famously said, 'All truly great thoughts are conceived by walking.' So, when you need ideas, take a walk in the park closest to your office, or a walk around your office block after lunch while talking at leisure. Maybe the much-maligned phrase 'Go take a walk' can now assume new and positive dimensions.

Unlocking Rhythm

If you have an office gym, try stationary cycling or some other form of light exercise.

If you are sitting in a long meeting, try light swinging of your legs in a rhythmic fashion. If you have a shower in office, utilize it when you need an idea. For many people, ideas drop into their minds when they are engaged in such rhythmic, routine activities that do not intensely involve the intellect. I have noticed colleagues who doodle meaninglessly during meetings, perhaps for the same reason. Rhythm appears to unlock the mind.

I get my best ideas while talking to colleagues informally over a nice cup of coffee.

19

What Your Wall Says about You on a Video Call

Some of the smaller pleasures and pain points of working from home.

In 2020, many of us began working from home, an experience we may never have had earlier. Our offices and social media educated us immediately and extensively on the etiquette of working from home. How to use online platforms, conduct video meetings, ergonomic seating at home, dealing with ambient noise including sounds created by children and pets, and the need to pace oneself well. So, when I wrote this piece in mid-2000, I really did not have much more to say on these work-from-home aspects.

I have, however, taken the opportunity to highlight some of the smaller pain points and pleasures of working from home, which have perhaps missed the attention of our overworked human resources team members during this unprecedented period.

Your Setting Defines You

In my first video meeting from home, I realized that the wall behind me had a backdrop of two ferocious-looking wooden face masks, which I had brought back from a visit to Korea many years ago.

I thought that wasn't appropriate at all, and certainly not in today's environment where masks are meant primarily to keep the virus out of your respiratory system. So, for my next Microsoft Teams video call, I prudently moved to another spot at home. But then I realized that the backdrop behind me now had two tall metal cats on a sideboard and a wall hanging with eight Japanese Gods depicted. A colleague on the other end told me politely that this was very distracting. On reflection, I agreed with him.

Two thin cats and eight strange gods is a little too much, by any standard. So, eventually, I moved to another location, where there was a plain white wall behind me, with absolutely nothing on it. So far, that's worked well, and I feel quite professional once again.

Therefore, I would recommend a plain, neutral backdrop when you do video calls from home. The main lesson here is, be aware of that wall behind you.

Spousal Distancing

Physical distancing is very important to keep the coronavirus away. What is equally important, for many of us who are not single, is adequate distancing from our spouse or partner, through our working day. This is because, notwithstanding all the love and affection we may have for each other, it is rather difficult for partners or spouses to be with each other, or cohabit and work in a single room, twenty-four hours a day.

Your voice begins grating on each other's nerves, your offices begin spilling into each other, and you cannot rule out occasional emotional outbursts that can upset the steady environment required for work. So, my data scientist wife now uses the study table, and I use the dining table. Or vice versa, on some days. We are at a comfortable distance from each other during the day, and then we meet again by 6 p.m., once we have logged off from our respective workplaces. Small homes may make a significant degree of separation difficult to achieve, but then, we are Indians and we know how to adjust.

Making Coffee and Tea

One of the first work-from-home truths I realized was that good coffee and tea are essential for our brains to switch on and work well. Many of our offices serve us excellent freshly brewed coffee, and some offices have gone to the extent of installing exotic fresh bean coffee machines with multiple Italian-style options. Frankly, our offices have spoilt us with all this choice because when I tried my hand at brewing some fresh coffee at home on my first work-from-home day, it turned out to be weak and watery. On the second try, it became milky and syrupy. Eventually, I got myself a nice big jar of freeze-dried instant coffee from the supermarket, diligently followed the instructions on the label and made a reasonably good cup. I have now realized that trying to brew fresh coffee at home is an art, and unless you know it well and have all the right equipment with you, it is best to stick to making simple instant coffee. Similarly, to make some good tea quickly, between your online calls, the safe and fast option is the teabag. Don't even try teapots and brewing unless you have prior experience and at least fifteen minutes at hand. The hard truth from this experience is that we take our workplace coffee and tea for granted.

Gossip, Grapevine and Murmurs

Most of my online calls have been productive, and the whole work-from-home system appears to be settling down well, when viewed through the narrow lens of work output. What I miss, though, is the buzz of office, including the gossip. How do you replicate this at home? Can online chats serve this purpose, even remotely? What is the work-from-home equivalent of the chatter at the water-cooler or in the corridor? My recommendation here is to relax a little during lunchtime and call your close office colleagues or friends in the time-tested, old-fashioned way, over the telephone. If possible, even try a personal conference chatter call among some of you and try to replicate a little bit of the informal office buzz on this call, before you switch back to serious work. It is important to have office fun while working from home.

I have realized that I snack far more often when I work from home. The pandemic may now have largely gone away, but I am still searching for a solution to this big fat problem.

20

The Joy of Using a Notebook

Your good old diary brings you so many benefits and it can also remain with you forever.

I began the New Year with a new work accessory—a notebook, gifted by my wife. The cover is a bright orange and the soft pages are bound nicely with thread.

What I have noticed since I started using this beautiful notebook made by the century-old Leuchtturm1917, is that I'm writing much more, jotting down things beyond routine notes and bullet points. It now contains several inspiring quotes, interesting and sometimes totally random ideas that occur to me during the day, and a number of intriguing doodles whose complexity is directly proportional to my boredom during some meetings.

I also confess that I love showing off the bright orange colour during Zoom calls and in regular meetings, secretly hoping it makes me look and feel younger and hipper than I actually am.

This has, in turn, made me reflect on the value that notebooks bring into our lives. Lost in the midst of notepads on our digital devices, many of us have abandoned paper notebooks, which I think has been to our general detriment.

Take a look at all these benefits notebooks can bring into our lives.

Instant Recorder

Notebooks help you record your thoughts the very moment they occur to you, and you can then keep playing with them, refining them as you go along. As Leuchtturm1917, the premium stationer, says, 'Cross them out, edit them, forget them, find them again, doodle around them, define them, revise them, make sketches, at your desk, on the train, up on a mountain, on a beach, in the bath, in bed.'

If you carry a small notebook and a pen wherever you go, you don't have to be worried about forgetting any useful idea that has struck your mind. Who knows when that crazy marketing plan or product idea may come of use? I have seen many CEOs and managers carry a small notebook with them for this very reason. Notebooks are the best antidote to forgetfulness.

A Creative Push

A notebook at your constant disposal encourages you to be creative. Empty pages welcome you to write prose or poetry in them. Most writers, including the growing tribe who aspire to write well, have their favourite notebooks.

If you are an architect or engineer or graphic designer, notebooks invite you to sketch your designs in them. If you are a scientist, you can use them to jot down your formulae and hypotheses. If you are in love, God bless you, you can use these pages to write out your secret notes of endearment, till you eventually muster up the courage to share them. I believe that the more simple or beautiful your notebook is, the more conducive it is to the flow of creative expression.

A Style Statement

A notebook is no longer just a book to write in, it's also a style statement.

A Moleskine in your hand, for instance, says something about you using the same brand that has been used by legendary artists and thinkers over the past 200 years, such as Pablo Picasso, Bruce Chatwin and Ernest Hemingway. On the other hand, a leather-bound Montblanc says something about your taste for avant-garde luxury products and the expensive, exclusive things in life. And should you choose to use India's own, relatively inexpensive Classmate or Navneet notebooks, that says something too— about the unpretentious simplicity that you prefer in life.

The colours you use, from a sedate black or dark blue to a flaming orange or purple, also make a statement for the kind of person you are or aspire to be. Whichever way you look at it, the 'notebook statement' is yours to make. Much like a wristwatch, pen or shirt, a notebook is yet another fashion accessory you can flaunt.

An Un-Digital Space

So much is going digital all around us that we sometimes desperately seek an 'un-digital' space to unwind in. Notebooks can provide a refuge because when you pick up your pen and write in one, you instantly transport yourself back in time to an old-fashioned world, where charm and elegance are more important than hotspots and Wi-Fi speed. What's more, with paper notebooks, you can be far more certain of the privacy of your writings, compared to the digital world, where we are constantly worrying about how all our data is getting shared with all and sundry. Another good thing about notebooks is their instant accessibility at all times—you don't have to wait for them to boot up, and neither do you need to get anxious that they will run out of battery in the next ten minutes.

Let me end with a final submission. Notebooks, like albums that contain printed photographs, have a sort of permanency to them. Digital devices and software tools are likely to get constantly upgraded and replaced every few years, and how this will impact all the content you have created and stored in them is rather unclear. But your good old notebook, with all your jottings, can remain with you forever, familiar and unchanged.

I think notebooks also have a nice, nostalgic effect. They take us back to our school and college days, which were some of the best times of our lives.

21

Hercule Poirot Can Solve Your Work Problems, Too

The famous detective can offer veritable masterclasses in the art of becoming a better, more efficient manager.

The legendary detective Hercule Poirot turned 100 in the year 2020. Created by 'Queen of Crime' Agatha Christie in 1920 in her first book, *The Mysterious Affair at Styles*, Poirot has an egg-shaped head with plenty of grey cells, a waxed moustache he's proud of, and a fetish for absolute order in everything he does. He solves every murder mystery he is presented with, using the powers of his great mind. Small wonder then that Poirot novels continue to be bestsellers, a full century after he burst on to the scene.

That's good news for the publishers but why should we, managers of the modern world, bother about Poirot stories or other detective novels? After all, our KRAs include finding answers to leading teams, understanding consumer behaviour, building robust processes, delivering sales growths—not solving crime.

Given this, you may well conclude that the most useful books to invest in are serious business tomes, not fun detective novels. I disagree. The same powers that detectives like Poirot employ to solve crimes can help us become far more effective managers in the offices. There is no mystery to this if you consider the following points.

Keep It Sharp

Great detectives observe the scene of the crime and human behaviour very carefully. They constantly pick up every small thing or event that is out of place—a second stain on a carpet, a book that is wrongly stacked or a man who appears too eager to talk but only at night. One or more of these small observations provides the detective with a clue to what could have really happened.

Well, that's true for managers too. If we observe our teams and workplaces carefully, notice a team member who is suddenly silent or a task that is slowly falling behind schedule, or a colleague who appears unduly harried, each of these deviations from the 'normal order' can provide us clues on what we can do to set things right. Sharp observation enables us to show empathy to colleagues. It helps us spot and curb wastages. Observing consumers closely throws up surprising insights that can lead to the next big idea. Detective novels bring to life some amazing methods of observation.

Data Alert

Poirot and other great detectives are excellent at spotting red herrings, which initially appear quite seductive, only to turn out that it was the criminal who planted them to lead people astray.

Similarly, in our own organizations, there is no dearth of red herrings that can lead us to entirely wrong conclusions. First and foremost, there is a deluge of data that reaches us from multiple physical and digital sources. Misinterpretation of such data, either consciously or inadvertently, is a big red herring we are faced with almost every day. Often, selective data is used to justify a wrong conclusion. How do detectives cast aside the red herrings that they come across and focus only on the essential information, which can then lead them towards the eventual truth? Detective novels are likely to provide you better pointers on this subject than any business book can.

The Right Question Wins

Brilliant detectives succeed in their quest for the truth because they ask the right questions. These questions may appear innocuous or stupid, but they are carefully designed to elicit information that helps complete the jigsaw puzzle. That's true of managers, too. Unless we ask the right questions, it is unlikely that we will get the right answers that will help us deliver growth, profitability or innovation. To do this well, we always need to have the larger jigsaw picture in mind. Our questions have to address the gaps we wish to fill in this picture instead of being merely led by the colourful PowerPoint slides in front of us. Detective novels, featuring greats like Poirot and Sherlock Holmes, are veritable masterclasses in the art of asking the right questions in the most disarming way.

Action and Reflection

When the famous detective Sherlock Holmes wishes to ruminate, he retreats into solitude and plays the violin or smokes his pipe.

Similarly, the shrewd old Jane Marple (another Agatha Christie creation), who solves many complex village crimes, engages in silent knitting as she reflects on everything she has seen and heard.

Detective novels bring home to us the need for reflection to solve difficult problems. As managers, we are often addicted to action—our familiar world of project meetings, email trails and action plans. But if we study the methods of Holmes and Poirot, we find that action and reflection need to happily co-exist to produce the required results. Reflection is not easy. It can be lonely and challenging. But, as Poirot will tell you, the grey cells need space and silence to work at their best.

A Clean Break

The simplest and the best reason to read detective novels is that they are so enjoyable. Most of us love a good murder mystery. We get absorbed in trying to solve the mystery ourselves, before the detective can. Most of the time our guesses are wrong, but this endeavour is so immersive that it takes our mind off our day-to-day stresses. That's a clean break we owe ourselves, particularly in these difficult times.

My idea for this piece came from my colleague Suparna Mitra, who works at Titan and loves detective novels. We worked together at Titan for several years, where we attempted to apply our detective skills to solving some of the mysteries of consumer behaviour and the marketing world.

22

Please Add Kindness to Your To-Do List as Well

To beat the blues, be kind to yourself, to those around you and to strangers.

We have now crossed over from the peak of the Covid-19 pandemic. While many of us are now toggling between office and home, some of us continue to work from home and many are at the frontlines. Most of us are doing our best to work hard and smart, and be as productive as we can.

Yet buried deep within us is the continuing stress of having lived through a pandemic—from the uncertainty of how long this madness would last, to the constant fear of job loss and the surreality of trying to get through a normal workday when few things around us were actually normal. The pandemic may now be largely over, but many other similarly stressful situations are likely to come upon us, from time to time. The best antidote to all this stress is kindness.

As David Hamilton highlights in his book, *The Five Side Effects of Kindness*, kindness makes us happier because it elevates the levels of dopamine in our brains. And I think that when we are happy, we are able to breathe freely, think creatively and make the most of what is available to us. This is true at all times, but particularly important during this unusual period.

If kindness is the best stressbuster, what can we do to be kind to ourselves and to the people around us every single day? I am not talking of large acts of kindness or generosity, which are of course welcome, but of everyday kindness, which each of us can practise. Here are some thought starters on this subject.

Home Vacation, Anyone?

Being kind to oneself is the first stop because if you are not kind to yourself, then it is unlikely you can be genuinely kind to others.

The most important type of self-kindness is to recharge one's body and mind on a regular basis, so that we are not constantly struggling to get through the day. This requires you to eat and sleep well. Take an hour off every afternoon for a good lunch break, dwelling on the pleasures of eating a nice meal.

Take a walk outdoors each evening to feel the spring in your step. Set yourself a firm deadline by when to start and end work each day, even if you are working from home. Take a 'home-vacation' break occasionally.

We owe it to our co-workers to work hard and contribute well during this difficult time. But equally, we also owe it to ourselves to rejuvenate ourselves, else there's a strong possibility that we may burn out before the pandemic does.

Creativity Has Its Perks

One of the easiest forms of kindness that you can show yourself is to make time for your creative passions regularly. Given the constraints of this pandemic, try to focus on a passion that you can indulge in within the four walls of your home. If you are keen on nature and gardening, nurture a small balcony garden in your home. If you love painting, there is no better time than now to dabble with your canvases and paintbrushes. If you enjoy baking or experimenting with new foods, why not start right away? If you enjoy writing, spend a few minutes journaling each day.

Being creative gives us the feeling of being free. This freedom releases us, at least momentarily, from the shackles of all our pandemic stress.

It's Okay, Say 'No'

One of the best ways to be kind to your work and team is to meet your work commitments. Make only the commitments that you can keep, given the multiple demands of the pandemic. Prioritize ruthlessly. Wherever possible (and this may not always be possible), say no to work that you don't have the clear bandwidth to take up.

But do remember that once you commit, one or more of your colleagues will soon be awaiting your end of the assignment, because their own work is perhaps dependent on it. When you complete your task on time, you eliminate their stress and you are, therefore, being kind to them. This is particularly important when people are isolated in their remote workplaces.

Make a 'Human' Call

People have been going through various unusual events and situations in their lives ever since the pandemic began. Transactional Zoom calls, for all their technological brilliance and attractive backdrops, are unlikely to tell us what exactly is happening in our colleagues' lives.

Given that we may not meet each other so regularly in office these days, we may never know that a teammate's close relative is still suffering from the effects of long Covid-19 or that her spouse, who lost his job during the pandemic, has still not found one that is right for him. Perhaps the best way to be kind, in this context, is to engage in human conversations with one or two colleagues every day, talking not about work, but about life in general. Receiving such a 'human' call from our boss, or our colleague, makes us feel valued as human beings. And knowing our colleagues' life context also then enables us to display genuine empathy in our everyday work. Kindness is really just a phone call away.

Surprise Works Too

When we wake up every morning, a good question to ask is, how can I be kind to someone, including myself, today?

Sometimes, kindness is at its best when it is unplanned. Be kind to yourself by taking out five minutes in the morning or evening to meditate. Or decide to drive out with your partner, family or friends with a packed lunch on a surprise picnic in that beautiful park you like so much. Reach out to a few elderly colleagues or relatives, and speak to them about their day, particularly if you sense they are experiencing loneliness. Call a team member and tell them how proud you are of the work they did the previous week. Share an appropriate inspirational quote or story with a friend who is recovering from illness or just like that.

Every random act of kindness is a win-win event; it makes both you and the person on other side of the phone feel good during this difficult time, and we go back to our work desks with happiness in our hearts.

My colleague Suparna Mitra of Titan helped provide valuable inputs for this article. Quite coincidentally, she was thinking about kindness around the same time I began reflecting on this subject.

23

Old-School Charm at Work

Some irreverent ideas to help you become a 'distinguished manager of substance'.

Over the past few years, offices have loosened their dress codes considerably. No longer are formal trousers and neatly ironed shirts required in our cubicles. Neckties, suits and saris are seen but rarely. Shocking bright colours have replaced light and sober tones, in dress and in office decor. Neatly combed hair and tidy cubicles are passé.

All this has happened for the ostensible purpose of encouraging creativity, productivity and an overall sense of libertarian happiness—though it is entirely unclear if those objectives are being met.

On the other hand, what is clear is that workspaces have begun resembling Woodstock. Often, there is just no way you can visually tell apart a learned marketing manager from the lead guitarist of a punk rock band.

Cubicles resemble cluttered junkyards of useless bric-a-brac. I believe that all this degeneration of office gravitas will just not do because it takes away from the ordered and civilized environment we require for sound decision-making and serious official interaction. For instance, how can you even begin discussing a million-dollar deal with a man dressed in frayed jeans, a pink T-shirt and a slicked-back ponytail?

Below are eight bright and easy steps to becoming a distinguished manager of substance. Of course, these are in addition to the act of wearing an elegant dress to work, which sets the basic tone. Take your pick.

1. Wear Suspenders

    If you are an investment banker, red suspenders are the right choice. If you are a sales manager, try black ones. An added functional advantage is that suspenders hold up trousers very secretly, so you are unlikely to be caught with your pants down.

2. Sport a Huge Solitaire

    For women executives, a huge diamond on the ring finger works wonders at all times. It's a symbol of distinction and seriously, a two-carat shimmering rock cannot be ignored by anyone, particularly in an opening handshake. And if you can wear two of them, one on each hand, you are home, lady.

3. Use Business Books Effectively

    There are hundreds of business books these days that claim to teach you the skills of effectiveness, execution and leadership. We are not suggesting that you read all these books as we are good folks and would not like to subject you to such cruelty. However, you must buy a few of these wonderful books and display them in your cubicle. That marks you out as a distinguished and intelligent manager, immediately. Thick, hard-bound tomes written by legendary names such as Peter Drucker and Alfred Chandler work the best. To draw attention to these books, you could even loan them to visitors.

4. Pursue a Doctoral Degree
    The ultimate passport to becoming a DIMS is a doctoral degree. Let us quickly clarify that you don't need to qualify for a PhD (which can be very strenuous), you just need to enrol for one. Then you can actually say heavy-duty things like: 'I am in the midst of doctoral research, on eight new ways of creating a winning strategy' or 'My doctoral guide at Harvard suggests I link the ideas of Sigmund Freud to the evolution of post-modern leadership styles'. You will make an immediate impact. And if you actually get lucky and earn a PhD, people will always have to address you as 'Doctor so-and-so', which will offer you lifelong gravitas.

5. Wear Golden Cufflinks
    Cufflinks are a mark of impeccable and superior style. They show other executives and visitors that you have taken care to dress well, that you belong to a polished elite. For special effect, use cufflinks with engraved monograms on them, which will leave everyone wondering which exclusive society or club you are part of.

6. Speak Very Softly
    Loud voices are for the streets and shouting is for boors. If you wish to be a distinguished manager, you must speak

softly, very softly. That's what sets apart the ladies and gentlemen from brash young upstarts. Don't worry if your voice dips from hushes tones from time to time, and you are asked to repeat yourself. That will give you the additional time to think before you speak. There is also an unintended bonus of soft speech—at a later date, you can actually deny that you said something, claiming that you were not heard properly.

7. Drink Earl Grey Tea
    Drink and serve Earl Grey tea in your office. This is the intellectual's cuppa and positions you well above the drinkers of masala chai. You must inhale the aroma, gently sip the black tea and then add just a dash of milk. Make sure you get your tea in white bone china cups, and forbid the use of those horrible, colourful mugs with senseless messages on them which seem to have taken over our offices.

8. Grow a Well-Kept Beard
    A nicely trimmed, well-shaped beard positions you immediately as a manager who is experienced and wise. If the beard is of neat and clean proportions, with not a single hair sticking out of length, it also shows the world that you are meticulous in your habits. When you want to appear particularly thoughtful, you should stroke your beard softly and look out into empty space. That always works.

I think the best route to becoming a distinguished manager of substance is to roll up your sleeves and produce consistent, excellent results at work.

24

What If Working from Home Goes on Forever?

Small human touches that can recreate joys of the office while working from home.

As the aftermath of the Covid-19 pandemic leads more companies to consider remote working as their new reality, keeping the human touch alive in our interactions with colleagues by making that extra effort to crack a joke or praise someone becomes more important than ever before

As offices begin reopening in the aftermath of the pandemic, a debate has arisen over the merits of working from home versus returning to office. While many companies are of the view that employees should return to office, some companies are offering a hybrid model whereby employees can work for two days a week from the comfort of their home. And there are a few companies which have made work from home a permanent feature.

Now, that's not too bad at all, say some of my friends, because WFH saves on precious commuting time. Productivity has also gone up ever since employees have begun working from home, as there are none of the silly distractions of office, say proponents of WFH. Some other friends believe all this short-term productivity has only been made possible because we know our colleagues well, and have built strong bonds with them by working together for years. That social capital can sustain a few months of WFH and transactional video calls, and then we will need to be back in our offices for sure, they say.

Even while this interesting debate runs its course, there is one aspect of work from home that we would do well to pay heed to—the human touch, which can bring in the fun and happiness of our offices into our homes. I am not talking here of knowledge webinars or online learning programmes, which are no doubt important because they keep us engaged intellectually.

I am talking of recreating the joys of offices, and banishing the loneliness that often accompanies WFH, with little touches that we often forget. Here are a few of them.

Make Time for Corridor Talks

Spontaneous corridor conversations are such a wonderful part of office life. You meet a colleague on your way to the staircase or pantry, or you drop in at their workstation on a whim, and you get around to immediately discussing something which has been on your minds. These are unplanned meetings, but I think we look forward to them.

WFH, because everyone is remote, tends to be much more planned, with meetings that are scheduled well in advance. You can break this well-scheduled, rigid pattern by calling a colleague spontaneously, at lunchtime or at the end of day, just to talk about something that needs a little bit of smart navigation, or to pick each other's brains about some unique problem that needs resolution. Such spontaneous calls are so different from scheduled and well-planned video meetings that they trigger a different channel in our minds, and leave us fulfilled in a nice and charming way.

Sit Back and Relax

Having coffee and tea together with your teammates is one of the most relaxing rituals at office. This is also the time for banter and light conversation. Some teams prefer to do this in the mornings and others in the late afternoons.

You can bring this joyful coffee break into your WFH routine too by scheduling virtual coffee breaks with your colleagues over a video call, once or twice a day. Switch on the video, see each other, sip your cups of coffee and chat for a while. Stay off serious work topics during virtual coffee time. But irreverent references to the workplace or poking a bit of fun at yesterday's virtual meetings are totally in order.

Humour Always Helps

Offices and conference rooms come alive when there's a touch of humour in the air. When we take a break during a meeting in the office, there's often humorous banter that goes around. Some colleagues are naturally more humorous and they ensure meetings do not get too uptight, boring or serious. There is a tendency for meetings over video to be largely devoid of humour, because everyone is focused on productive conversation and the transaction at hand. It is also easier to be humorous when you are all together, in person.

You can address these deficiencies by injecting some WFH humour yourself into a few remote meetings that you are part of—particularly with teammates whom you know well. Towards the end of any such remote team meeting, request your colleagues to switch on their video feeds, and one or two of you can then narrate a small humorous incident each from your homes. You will be in for a jolly laugh or two as your colleagues begin sharing amusing anecdotes of their goof-ups in the kitchen or while keeping an eye on the kids.

Go Ahead, Appreciate Your Peers

Often caught in our own WFH warp, we focus on being very productive and forget to convey our appreciation for others' achievements, however small or big.

Providing and receiving genuine appreciation is one of the best points of office life, and this should never take a back seat, even while working remotely. In offices we see our colleagues regularly and so we are able to convey our thanks or praise in person. When we work from home, we hardly meet them personally. So, it is useful to make a mental note of any achievement that strikes you as commendable, and then send your colleague a message of generous admiration for what she or he has been able to deliver. Remember that this is still the aftermath of a pandemic and a crisis, that people are working with anxieties about their health and families. Hence, taking the extra effort to share a word of praise, even for a small accomplishment, is worthwhile during these difficult times.

I try to bring a human touch to my WFH routine by engaging in arguments on video calls; arguing, after all, is so human.

25

Seven Habits of Very Happy Managers

Short presentations, saying no to multitasking and making weekend plans—here are some ways to keep a smile on your face.

Stephen Covey, one of the most admired management gurus of modern times, passed away a few years ago. Most of us have read his bestseller, *The 7 Habits of Highly Effective People*. Thousands of people have claimed that this book has changed their lives and careers forever.

Here, I pay a simple but irreverent tribute to this influential thinker, on behalf of all office goers. I believe it is important for managers to be both happy and effective. Since Covey has already revealed how we can be highly effective, I tell you what it takes to be very happy at work. Just follow the seven simple habits described below, and you will smile every day.

First Things First, Eat a Good Lunch

As Covey says, we must put first things first. Therefore, a good and relaxed lunch in office takes the highest priority. Without it, you can never really be happy. If you hurry through this essential meal or skip it, you are likely to find yourself in a grumpy mood throughout the afternoon and evening. Your stomach may begin grumbling and you may end up eating too many fat-laden cookies during the rest of the day, which is not good for your waistline or your heartline. On the other hand, a delicious and healthy lunch, had with colleagues, with a good measure of talk and laughter, is a recipe for good cheer.

Begin with the Weekend in Mind

Covey's book advises us to always begin with the end in mind. We modify this advice slightly, and urge you to begin with the weekend in mind. The weekend is an enduring source of happiness, and therefore deserves a lot of attention and planning. Have you made a booking at that Thai spa? Have you decided where to party hard, and with whom? What about dinner with your glamorous ex-girlfriend, who has hinted that she wants to get back in touch with you? If your boss is in a generous mood, could you request him for an off day either on Friday or Monday, thereby creating an extra happy and long weekend? These are just a few of the many complex weekend choices we are faced with, so clearly we have to begin preparations in earnest by Monday morning.

Keep Your Presentations Brief

We must recognize that no one, not even the chairperson, wants to attend a long and serious PowerPoint presentation these days, when there are many other interesting office pastimes to pursue.

So, if you have to think win-win, your presentations must never exceed five slides and must conclude in ten minutes flat. You will find that most things can be summarized within that length and time. Also, your boss will be so happy with the quick ending that he is likely to approve your budgets immediately. If you want to deliver true happiness, begin and end your presentation with an appropriate comic strip visual which makes people smile. That will leave just three slides for the serious stuff, which is just about perfect.

Silence Is Really Golden

Managers love talking at meetings, and this is what gets them into deep trouble in the first place. So, you are likely to be the happiest if you keep as silent as possible, unless you have dramatic views that can potentially change the course of your company's history. Let others in the room argue and fight among each other, while you remain, like the Buddha, calm and composed amid the gathering storm. Take copious notes, but don't speak. Once in a while, look up, smile and nod enigmatically at the people who are doing the talking. They will regard these gestures as signs of deep wisdom and understanding.

Engage in Healthy Gossip

Scientific studies have consistently revealed that cubicle gossip is a great source of happiness. If you are a creative individual, you can actually be the source of some gossip. Otherwise you can choose to merely be a conduit for the grapevine. Either way, you are adding to the HQ (happiness quotient) of your office, which is so important in these stressful times. The conference room, email, water cooler, lift, office loo—they are all perfect locations for such talk. There is a caveat to be borne in mind, though. Healthy gossip has boundaries which need to be respected.

Don't Multitask

Many managers think they must display their professional manhood by engaging in several activities at the same time. They believe multitasking is essential, given the multiple demands at the modern workplace. They also feel good that they are intellectually competent enough to do many things at once. Don't believe in such rubbish. Multitasking is a recipe for being short of breath throughout the day, which, as we know, leads to hypertension and all its attendant ailments. In addition, it ensures that none of the jobs you are doing ever receive your full attention, leading to a state of niggling unhappiness at all times. To be really happy at the workplace, address one job at a time, and do it really well. By doing this, you may complete fewer tasks during the day, but you will leave the office with a spring in your step.

Refresh and Renew Yourself

Covey speaks about the need for reflection and for renewing yourself, the last of the seven habits he prescribes. This habit is as important for happiness as it for effectiveness. Unless you give yourself time every day to think and relax, you will never really be happy with yourself. There are many practical methods to achieve this. Define daily digital blackout periods, when you will not go anywhere near a computer or a mobile phone. Pursue a creative passion outside the workplace—this could range from painting (which is generally safe) to music (which may be dangerous if you are a bad singer and sing in public). Take time out to run or play tennis or work out in the gym, and use this time to blank out your busy mind. Finally, don't meet or speak to your boss for at least two days each week, and see for yourself how completely this relaxes your entire being.

I think the eighth and most important habit of very happy managers is our ability to laugh at ourselves, which is the first step to having great fun at work.

26

What the Dickens?

Did you know that many characters from the books of Charles Dickens inhabit our offices?

Most of us are familiar with Charles Dickens, one of the greatest writers of all time. Many of us have grown up reading his novels—*Great Expectations, Oliver Twist, A Christmas Carol* and *A Tale of Two Cities*. We easily recognize his colourful gallery of characters as they walk the grimy streets and workhouses of Victorian England. What is, however, not well-known is that the characters created by Charles Dickens are not confined to his books. They live in our modern-day offices, where we meet them daily. I pay an irreverent tribute to the great master by casting a quick look at the Dickensian cast that inhabits the cubicles next to ours.

Oliver Twist

Probably the best-known character in all of Dickens' stories, this young orphan boy famously 'asks for more', a pitiful request for more soup, which is treated with derision and scorn by Mr Bumble, the pompous master of the orphanage. We are all Oliver Twists of the modern office era (well, at least most of us are). We constantly desire and ask for more—higher salary, additional perks, more international travel, more manpower and bigger budgets. Our senior management plays its role of Mr Bumble to the hilt. There are many twists to this recurring tale, though the ending is similar in most cases: We find ourselves in the soup with little response to our requests, and we continue to bumble around.

The Artful Dodger

Oliver Twist's friend, the Artful Dodger, is famous for 'never getting caught', for always dodging upholders of the law. We recognize very well the Artful Dodgers of our offices. They never seem to complete their work or meet their targets, yet they take it easy, plan plenty of time off, have a glib response to all queries and never get caught by their bosses. Sometimes a few of us may detest them, but mostly we admire their skills of evasion and their teflon-coated tongues. And, of course, we wonder why our bosses fall for them.

Wilkins Micawber

This memorable character from the novel *David Copperfield* is constantly in debt and penury, yet he is the eternal optimist, hoping that 'something will turn up' to resolve all his problems. To paraphrase Mr Micawber, 'I have no doubt I shall begin to live in a perfectly new manner, if—if, in short, something turns up.' We know many colleagues in office who share this philosophy. They live in the constant hope that something or someone will turn up tomorrow to help them meet their deadlines, achieve their targets or delight their departmental heads, all of which appears totally impossible at the moment. With this fond Micawberian hope in their heart, and entirely unable to cope with the present, they promptly leave early for the day.

Ebenezer Scrooge

Scrooge is featured in *The Christmas Carol* as a cold-hearted, greedy, miser. He despises all things that give people happiness. He speaks in a grating voice and treats his employees shabbily. It is unfortunate that many corporate bosses of today have chosen him as a role model. Like Scrooge, they are consumed by a desire to make big profits for their enterprises. As they walk down Scrooge's path, they scrutinize expense statements with electron microscopes and they cut our budgets for a million reasons. More sadly, they serve second-rate liquor at corporate get-togethers which leave us with awful hangovers. To be fair, not all bosses are followers of Scrooge—some of them do occasionally smile.

Mr Pickwick

He is the lead character of *The Pickwick Papers*, and he researches the quaint and curious phenomena of life. This takes him into several interesting and unpredictable adventures. Blessed are the Pickwicks in our offices. They delve into the curious phenomena of others' lives and then tell us all about their juicy findings.

They lovingly tend to our office grapevine, and they believe (as we do, too) that cubicle gossip about quaint and scandalous stuff is the ultimate chicken soup for the corporate soul. They break the monotony of our working days, so may their tribe increase.

Joe, the Fat Boy

Joe is a minor companion and the attendant of Mr Pickwick. He is heavyset, consumes great quantities of food and can fall asleep at any time of the day. We are not piqued by his physique but by his boundless capacity for sleep. We wonder how some executives in our offices can manage to sleep through virtually every meeting or conference and wake up just in time for the concluding round of snacks. They have mastered the art of sleeping while sitting upright, with their eyes parted just enough to thwart suspicion. They pretend to be listening but suddenly, as you are winding up a long presentation, they will exclaim— 'What was that you just said? I didn't get you, could you go over it once more, if you don't mind?' We know exactly how you feel at that moment.

Mr Jaggers

This prominent London lawyer appears in the pages of *Great Expectations*. Mr Jaggers is an important man and privy to dirty business. One of his distinguishing features is that his hands always smell of carbolic soap, because he keeps washing them obsessively. This he does to rid himself of the taint of the clients that he interacts with. Some executives in our offices pick up this habit quite naturally. They are always busy washing their hands of several matters. Sometimes, they disown their own work and always know just whom to blame for various failures. Of course, they quickly disassociate themselves with projects that are headed downhill.

My cubicle philosophy is simple: Achieving targets and deadlines is necessary, but it is equally important to have a Dickens of a time.

27

An Office Worker's Guide to the Zodiac

What does the year ahead have in store for you? Let the sun signs speak.

Experts have used the zodiac to predict matters such as love and relationships, success and failure. But this piece will fill an important knowledge gap in an area oft-neglected by soothsayers: a zodiac guide for office workers like you and me. After all, we absolutely need to know what will happen to our colleagues and us in the new year. What does the year have in store for you? We take a rather liberal and flexible view towards sun signs, so you don't have to restrict yourself to your own conventional sign of the zodiac. Go ahead and choose any of these twelve predictions for 2023, based on your innermost desire. Please also note that while this essay refers to 2023, it remains equally valid for any other year.

Let us begin with some Confucian office philosophy. 2023 is the Chinese Year of the Rabbit. A stark contrast to 2022, which was the Year of the Tiger. This is then definitely a year of great contrasts.

Capricorn: With a goat as your sun sign, will you be a sacrificial lamb in office? Or will you finally get your boss's goat in the new year? Either way, we predict you will obtain a salary increase which may not fully satisfy your insatiable craving for luxury goods. During the year, a colleague may try to occupy your cubicle without your permission. You must resist this fiercely, unless the colleague is a hot young dragon of the opposite sex.

Aquarius: This is the most masculine of sun signs, savour the power. You may have occasional trouble with some members of your team but remember that most things can be resolved over a few delicious vodka shots at the end of the day. Be extra courteous to the liftman and pantry boy, because they are essential to cubicle-happiness.

Pisces: You are a child of the sea, so you must head to the beach for regular breaks from office. In 2023, you have the choice to be a bloodthirsty shark, a playful dolphin or even a fish out of water. Even as you exercise this choice, here is a startling prediction: you are likely to shorten all your office emails to crisp one-liners, which may establish a welcome new global trend.

Aries: This year (like most years in most offices) will be the best and the worst of times. You will be bold in your actions, like the battering ram which is your sun sign. For instance, you may approach your boss for an out-of-turn double promotion. You will not fret over small matters. Instead, you will lose sleep over big things which also will not matter in the long run.

Taurus: This is an interesting sun sign for a year of likely recession, because when everything is looking bearish, the bulls always shine. You will take extremely bullish postures on sales growths and interest rates, until everyone else including your banker tempers your posture. A big travel bug will bite you, but equally large cuts in your company's travel budget will be a terrible constraint.

Gemini: You will approach the year with twin objectives—meeting all of your office deadlines during the year and losing lots of weight. We caution you that both are impossible to achieve. Be pragmatic, set yourself simple and feasible goals such as leaving office promptly by 6 p.m. each evening, and enjoy the glorious year ahead.

Cancer: This sun sign spells competitive behaviour in office; haven't we heard of all those crabs dragging each other down? You will compete for the really big prizes, and you could end up either on the victory podium or in the Doctor's chambers, or in both places. Frankly, we think mountains and resorts are better destinations, and regardless of the prize you are pursuing, health should always take priority.

Leo: A year of many meetings awaits you, where your bosses roar endlessly, and long presentations are made forever. All is not lost, though. An interesting seminar in London or Paris may come your way, which will provide you an excellent opportunity to visit a few interesting museums or watch English Premier League football. When you return, call a half-day workshop to present your findings.

Virgo: We envy you, because this is the sun sign of office romance in 2023 and most other years too. Will you find your dusky soulmate amongst the new batch of incoming management trainees or perhaps in the dull corridors of the internal audit department? So, begin the year by checking out your company's rules on this delicate subject.

Libra: The career move you have always sought will hang in the balance, as headhunters contact you but don't come forward with firm offers. You are likely to get a new boss during the year. However, based on empirical evidence, we cannot assure you that this change will be for the better. You may be left pining for old times.

Scorpio: You enter the new year at your own risk, watch out for that sting in the tail. We fear that the start-up you are working for may suddenly announce significant downsizing, but this is not at all abnormal in a volatile year. Alas, this may be a poor year ahead, so be prepared to drown your sorrows.

Sagittarius: Strange and unbelievable things will happen to you this year. You will achieve and overtake your sales and other targets with ease, month after month. Your office notes and presentations will be hailed as masterpieces of communication. You will complete all work well ahead of schedule, which will give you enough time to party constantly. On that note of optimism and cheer, we wish all cubicle dwellers a fabulous year full of levity, fun and joy!

I prefer sunshine over sun signs, and fortune over fortune-telling. I assume no responsibility whatsoever for the veracity of predictions contained in this article.

28

How Often Do You Praise Others?

*Recognizing and saluting others' achievements is
good for you.*

In today's corporate world, we are generally very good at singing
our own praises. In fact, this is not just another corporate habit,
it is turning out to be a dominant trait of most managers today.
We like to highlight our achievements and many of us excel at
it. Look at the tens of thousands of social media posts all around
us (including some of my own) which showcase the winning
of some award or recognition. Since there is no dearth of such
awards, the potential for self-adulation is infinite.

In addition, many of us also take the time to recognize
members of our respective teams because we believe that this
is the right thing to do and helps reinforce good work and
morale. This is indeed important. Our organizations should
know what we have been up to, particularly the positive aspects
and notable successes. Acknowledging genuine achievements,
however small or big, is helpful and a practice that deserves
reinforcement.

But how often do we recognize and salute people who are outside our teams or who work in other companies, for accomplishments that we truly admire? How many posts or blogs have you seen calling out a milestone or a great success achieved by another company, or by a peer who you may regard as your professional rival? How often do we salute organizations and brands other than our own for brilliant work that we secretly wish we had done ourselves?

The answer is, very rarely. Great sportspersons and artistes do this sometimes but unfortunately, this has not been the way of the corporate world. While I have not researched the underlying reasons, there is bound to be strong rationale behind this behaviour, including ego, professional or personal jealousy and even a perception that this may not quite be the right thing to do.

However, there are many reasons why occasionally praising others, particularly for notable achievements, is a good and useful practice.

Self-Improvement

Inculcating this practice opens our mind to the fact that there are also others out there who are doing great things. This breaks insular thinking and delivers a reality check on the inflated opinion that many of us may carry about ourselves. Such a reality check can be a great trigger for self-improvement and is also a wonderful starting point for cultivating true humility.

Breaking Biases

Recognizing or saluting a competitor for any specific and significant success is also a great way of rising above professional jealousy or rivalry to acknowledge truly outstanding work. When we do this, it also helps us break other biases that we may hold about that person or company. And when we break such biases, we become far more open to studying their methods and what has contributed to their successes.

Enhancing Positivity

Praising another person is also a sign of our own self-assurance. People who are confident in their own capabilities are far more likely to call out the achievements of others. On the other hand, our inability or unwillingness to acknowledge others' successes is often a reflection of our own insecurities. I would also hypothesize that, provided we are reasonably good at what we do, we can grow in confidence by saluting superb work done by others. The very act enhances how positively we feel about ourselves.

A Cycle of Mutual Respect

Offering genuine praise to a colleague or friend for an achievement is also seen as a mark of respect for their capabilities, and a sign that you are choosing to recognize their strengths over their weaknesses. This can potentially set off a virtuous cycle of mutual respect as your colleague also chooses to reciprocate and recognize your own good work, thus building a source of excellent continuing motivation for both of you as you pursue new goals.

Growing Your Network

This is also an excellent way of growing your network in your industry. The person whose achievement you have highlighted is quite likely to become positively disposed towards you. In addition, the act of praising someone else, if it is authentic, is always seen as a gracious gesture, and most of us like to associate with people who are graceful. If, on the other hand, you are viewed as a person who is always talking exclusively about their own glorious deeds, it is unlikely that you will gain too many friends who are keen be part of your network.

Many Ways to Praise

Recognizing another team in your own company or a person who works in a different group or even a competitor can take many forms. Sometimes, a simple word of congratulations in the office corridor or on the sidelines of an industry conference is all that is required. At other times, a pleasant WhatsApp message or commendatory email can be encouraging. There may be the occasional moment when you wish to publicly praise the person or organization during a team meeting, a Town Hall or in a social media post. In my own experience, the right format depends on the context and the nature of the achievement you are calling out.

Whichever format and occasion you choose, do think about the central message of this piece: that praising others is good for you.

I would like to acknowledge the excellent and thoughtful inputs I have received for this piece from my colleague Suparna Mitra of Titan, who thinks deeply about how to build better workplaces and teams.

29

Conference 101—and Ways to Add Some Fun

There are many methods to enhance the fun and happiness quotient of conferences.

Conferences are a regular feature of modern corporate life. There are many diverse types: sales meets, marketing seminars, strategy summits, manufacturing symposia and so on. Undoubtedly, they add to productivity, profitability, team morale and success, else why would companies splurge huge amounts on hosting these shindigs?

I have little advice to offer on the serious content of conferences (that bit is best left to our bosses), but have plenty of ideas on how the fun and happiness quotient of these events can be significantly enhanced. In fact, a key objective of any conference should be fun, because none of us really wants to see hundreds of blank faces at the meets we attend. So here are some useful rules for you to read, and to send across to the relevant folk within your company.

Limit Serious Work to Three Hours

In any conference, the serious content includes the likes of keynote addresses, impressive presentations and panel discussions. Such vital but solemn content should cumulatively not exceed three hours, in any event. There is a simple basis for this conclusion. If the best of movies, with all their scintillating actors and emotive appeal, cannot hold our attention for more than three hours at a stretch, do heavy-duty speeches and PowerPoints delivered by corporate men and women really have a hope in succeeding beyond this time limit?

Choose a Bohemian Location

For creating a conference that everyone looks forward to, the location should be a strong antithesis to the serious demeanour of our cubicles. Budgets may limit specific choices here, but excellent locations—whether you choose extravagantly exotic South America, expensively chic Europe or just good old India—always have a liberating, bohemian feel to them. In contrast, cities with museums, cultural hotspots or theme parks have niche appeal. The ability to indulge in a relatively harmless but deliciously sinful activity, such as some minor gambling or a visit to a cabaret or a massage in a beach shack, always adds to the overall appeal of the location. The casinos of Macau or Las Vegas, the night spots of Bangkok and Pattaya, the punky streets of Rio and the beaches of Goa— take your pick.

Invite an Inspiring Speaker (Not from the Corporate World)

Conferences are worthless if they do not inspire the participants. But we know deep in our hearts that the business world has become increasingly staid and monotonous. Most speakers usually harp on topics like growth, productivity and financial returns. On the other hand, so much inspiring work today comes from the world of music, movies, art, adventure and sports. So, unless Steve Jobs or Richard Branson has agreed to address your conference, go ahead and invite an unconventional guest speaker or performer from one of these fields, someone who will elevate the audience. Two of the most memorable conferences I attended recently were a dialogue with a wealthy investor who spoke fearlessly, and a stand-up comedy performance which had everyone in stitches.

Concentrate on Food and Drink

When people come to conferences, they like to eat and drink shamelessly. Even conscientious dieters are known to let loose. This is a universal truth that organizers must bear in mind and feed generously. Great conventions have needlessly bitten the dust because the meal was not properly planned 'No Jain food, so we ate dry bread', 'A solitary vegetarian salad amid oceans of seafood', or 'Only one live pasta counter for 500 people, can you believe that' will be some of the brickbats flying your way. Serving up memorable food and drink at conferences requires imagination and balance, a perfect mix of the familiar and the adventurous. And even if you have the finest single malts and ice-vodka on tap, never forget the local brew; it always kicks in with a fiery ethnic touch.

Jam the Mobile Signals

Smartphones, smartwatches, iPads and other such marvellous modern devices transform promising conferences into noisy technological jungles. People are forever on the phone, conversing with their colleagues back in office, secretaries, spouses, maids, clients, headhunters, and God knows who else. To liberate participants guiltlessly from this trap, conference locations should jam all mobile signals. This is a proposition which will appeal to all because mobiles going off when an interesting speaker is on stage or while jiving on the dance floor can be quite annoying.

Organize a Rocking DJ and a Dance Floor

Nothing brings a conference alive like a rocking dance floor that parties boisterously into the night. To give the evening that special touch, have a party theme that is wild and fun. For real bonding to happen, everyone needs to let their hair down together, including senior and junior management, guests and every single participant. For this, you need a smart DJ who has a spontaneous feel for music that connects with your audience, so invest generously in such a man. You also need a location which does not impose draconian time limits that specify when all music and dance must shut down, or at the very least a place which displays flexibility in such critical matters. Of course, you also need a well-stocked bar, equipped with bartenders who can conjure up wicked blends quickly.

I have just returned from an exciting office conference in Goa and am thinking of the next one already. The charms of Goa are incomparable.

30

Monsters Inc.

Know the dementors who appear in our work lives and what to do about them.

Fans of Harry Potter know that dementors are fiends who suck out all our happiness, leaving us empty and forlorn. The final Harry Potter movie, which I first saw a long time ago and watched once again last month, has a generous helping of these monsters. Potter fights dementors with the powerful Patronus charm, the only magical spell which can dispel them.

All of us who dwell and work in office cubicles know that dementors are not fictional creatures because they appear in our work lives with depressing regularity. Here, I highlight a few office dementors and present powerful 'Cubiclus charms' with which you can battle them effectively.

A Bad Boss

A bad boss is the worst dementor of them all. He knows millions of foul ways to make your life miserable, and you often feel this is the overarching purpose of his life. He can yell at you, bug you, try to meddle in your work, refuse you the vacation you have been pining for, send you urgent work on a holiday and be unreasonable in a number of previously unimagined ways.

My Cubiclus charm: If you have a nasty boss, gift him tickets to the latest Harry Potter movie or buy him the DVD. Ask him to watch out for dementors in the film, tell him that he'll really like them because you think he is one of them. Stay at a safe distance from him for some days thereafter. When you return, you will know whether he has tried to transform himself (which is good) or whether it is time for you to move on (which, under the circumstances, may be a better decision).

Late-Evening Meetings

No dementor is eviller than one who calls meetings after 7 p.m. God intended all good people to be back home (or in other pleasant places) by this time. Even birds return to their nests by dusk. So, while family and friends are pining away, waiting for you at nightfall, you are listening to the boss challenging you to come up with new sales or production strategies to shore up the company's sagging bottom line.

My Cubiclus charm: Speak up right at the beginning of such meetings to make your presence felt. Provoke everyone by suggesting that the team should consider at least tripling sales in six months. This will delight your boss. Thereafter, slink out of the meeting very silently; if necessary, leave a notebook on the table to signal your continuing presence. To ensure an invisible exit, you should also seat yourself close to the door, and never next to the boss.

Extreme Air Conditioners

Wayward air conditioning can sometimes turn our offices into the Arctic Circle in deep winter or the Sahara Desert at high noon. Under these unfortunate dementor circumstances, you will either shiver or sweat profusely, and may even develop a migraine or mild pneumonia. With central air conditioning being the norm these days, you can't even switch off the blasted thing.

My Cubiclus charm: The best method to fend off extreme cold is a quick nip of brandy or vodka, if your office is the type that helpfully turns a blind eye to small hip flasks. Russians do this all the time. On the other hand, if it's uncomfortably warm, feel free to progressively unbutton your top-most garment or take off your shoes. Based on your age, sex, fitness and hygiene levels, this may provoke various interesting responses in the room, but anything is preferable to slow suffocation.

Elevators That Do Not Work

An office elevator that does not work is an early morning dementor. You can stare at it helplessly, kick the closed doors angrily or wait for a miracle that will suddenly make it work again. You can make suitable references to whoever is in charge of the elevators. All this activity, however, is likely to suck out whatever happiness you have begun the day with.

My Cubiclus charm: Don't wait for the lift to restart. Climb the stairs with a spring in your step, because every flight of stairs climbed is a few calories burned. Regard this as an opportunity for weight loss at no cost.

Tons of Unread Mails

In today's networked world, hundreds of unread emails in your inbox are dementors par excellence. You are never really sure what dangers lurk in these crowded cyber corridors, and you won't ever get time to read all these emails, let alone reply to them. Some emails are short, some long, some pictorial, others expressions of anguish—but generally, they all expect some sort of action or response from you. I have seen harried-looking executives assiduously work their emails in airports, on flights, at beaches, when all of us know that there are happier things to do at these lively locations.

My Cubiclus charm: Don't respond to all emails unless they are of direct or earth-shaking importance. Don't even bother reading various emails which are copied (marked cc) to you, if you find that these are sent for reasons which generally have nothing to do with you. If you are asked whether you have read that email from last week, request it to be re-sent to you. Keep an hour (and no more) aside each day to read and reply to emails and forget about them the rest of the time. Once a week, delete all pending mails in a single stroke, and inform your colleagues that you do this religiously.

I recommend two universal Cubiclus charms to stave off all dementors: good friends at work and reading this book from time to time.

31

The Geronimo Effect at Work

Simple tips to execute a few long-pending projects in office.

Project Geronimo, carried out by the US Navy Seals, lasted all of 40 minutes. That's the time it took for the commandos to arrive by helicopter in the dead of night, confront and kill Al-Qaeda leader Osama bin Laden in his lair at Abbottabad, Pakistan and take his body away for burial at sea.

I readily admit that office-goers like me are far from being navy seals or marines (just a glance in the mirror will dispel any illusions). But there are many 'Project Geronimos' we can implement in our workplaces—each project has the potential to make our workplaces cleaner and a lot more fun. Remember, it took the US ten long years to plan and execute the mission, but these tips that I am giving you below will take less than an hour and not much planning.

Clean Out That Cubicle

This is a top-priority Geronimo project. Empirical research, as well as my own shoddy experience in the matter, shows that you don't need more than 20 per cent of the stuff that clutters your cubicle and desk. Books, dusty files, assorted notes and post-its, historical photographs, magazines, dog-eared certificates, salary slips, pens that don't work, old mobile phones, airline tickets and boarding passes, ancient mouse pads . . . the random material that piles up and up on every horizontal surface in our cubicles is truly amazing in its scope and breadth of coverage. So, take forty minutes off your work today and clean up your cubicle. Be ruthless in identifying and throwing out the junk; you can give it a burial either at land or sea, based on where you are. You don't need helicopters for this and you will, of course, return every morning to a much cleaner cubicle.

Refresh Your Mind

An axiom of the modern workplace is that, as the day progresses, it keeps adding clutter and confusion to your mind. You can't do much about this. There are opinions and emails thrown at you, multiple things to be fixed, decisions to be made, numerous deadlines to be met, bosses to be met and lots more. My hunch is that the human mind is not designed to withstand such constant pressure for eight hours; it craves happiness, order and peace. So, a useful Geronimo project each day is to clean out your mind in just forty minutes. You can achieve this by taking a forty-minute walk with friends after lunch and talking about cabbages and kings. You can also achieve this by plugging in your iPod; I find that forty minutes of Pink Floyd purges my mind completely. As the wise men say, there are many such routes to nirvana; you have to choose your own. But you will come back to your workplace calmer, composed and more prepared to take on the rest of the mad long day.

Have That Long-Pending Conversation

Most of us have at least one long overdue chat in office which we have never got around to doing, but which hangs around like a tramp in the recesses of our mind. It could be something like clearing the air with a colleague over some recent incident or meeting a friend who has been waiting many days just to catch up. It could be a difficult conversation with your boss, telling him about things you absolutely don't like about your job, or what you really want to do in the future. All you need to do is take a Geronimo break from your work, and have this conversation today. The cappuccino is a good blend to bond over. If it's late evening, a glass of beer or wine will help the conversation flow.

Join the Slow Food Movement

One Project Geronimo we owe ourselves every day is a nice forty-minute lunch break away from our desks. For many of us, the lunch break has deteriorated into quickly gulping down whatever is on offer in the canteen, or a sandwich (or masala dosa, or our tiffin lunch) on our work desks. This is because we needlessly prioritize work over food, a highly undesirable habit born in productivity-obsessed countries. Learn from the French. Whatever be the pressing engagements at work, they take time off for a leisurely lunch, and return refreshed and energized. So, starting today, contemplate over your food, chew it slowly, enjoy the varied flavours at your canteen, ask for a second helping if you wish. Steadfastly refuse to answer phone calls during lunchtime, and don't even think of responding to text messages while eating. Indulge in an occasional dessert or ice cream which can re-energize your epicurean soul.

Fix Your Email

Unanswered mail in our inbox is the bane of our work lives. They cause a nagging anxiety, and ever so often, the accumulation reaches a point of no return, upon which we promptly and helplessly give up the chase. Mails from our bosses take precedence over those from our friends, and a mindboggling number of mails are copied to us for reasons we will never know. Do a quick Project Geronimo on this. To begin with, take forty minutes and clean out your inbox of all past emails. A good thumb rule is that any email message more than a month old is terribly outdated, and unlikely to be of any use to anyone. Thereafter, have a different Project Geronimo once a week. Keep aside forty minutes once a week (Friday evening is a good choice) to respond even briefly to emails from people who are important to you. Watch how good dialogues and friendships blossom once again.

I recently moved into a new cabin in my office block, and the forty-minute Project Geronimo I have launched to clear out all the junk is still very incomplete. Help from the US Navy Seals and anyone else is welcome.

32

And the Office Oscar Goes To . . .

Can we create some workplace awards that recognize simple,
good and welcome office behaviours?

Did you catch the Oscar ceremony on television when
it was broadcast earlier this year? If you did not, it doesn't
matter. Channels will occasionally broadcast highlights of the
event, and YouTube and online publications are likely to be
carrying colourful features where you can catch the famous
red carpet, beautiful bodies and designer gowns. But amid
all this Hollywood glitz and glamour, all of us who work
in offices strongly feel the need for our own Oscars. There
are tons of corporate awards for brilliant work performance,
exceeding sales targets, creating winning advertisements,
achieving excellent profits, but what we sorely lack are awards
that recognize simple, good and welcome behaviour in our
offices. The Office Oscars are being established for precisely
this purpose.

The 'Smiling Boss' Oscar

These days, bosses seldom smile, and they never do so on a Monday morning. You would also have noted a grim axiom: the bigger the boss, the smaller his or her smile until, like Alice's Cheshire Cat, the smile vanishes altogether. So, our first Office Oscar category is for the boss with the widest Monday smile. Just imagine how well you could kickstart the week if your biggest boss met you in the elevator today with a wide grin on his face. This may become infectious, because the entire office would end up smiling and whistling as we went about our work. Productivity would zoom. Nominees for this award should ideally also possess some sense of humour, and a self-deprecating wit. But we know we can't have everything, so we will happily settle for the smile alone.

The 'No PowerPoint' Oscar

PowerPoint presentations that are 100-plus slides long, with zillions of colourful charts, have replaced simple presentations on transparent acetates or well-written discussion papers, which used to make the essential points so well. Today's impressive-looking PowerPoint presentations obfuscate everything and are the ultimate victory of style over substance. To reverse this downward slide, we announce the No PowerPoint Oscar, to be given to the manager who shuns the use of PowerPoint presentations, and instead circulates a simple note which sets the basis for meaningful discussion at any meeting. At a stretch, managers who use PowerPoint but limit themselves to less than five slides per presentation can also apply for this award—this still represents good progress from the current morass.

The 'Cellphone Etiquette' Oscar

Nothing is more irritating than participants in a meeting constantly fidgeting with their mobiles or, even worse, busily typing into their smartphones while an important point is being desperately made. Our next category, therefore, honours the office colleague who refuses to touch his or her mobile phone during official meetings or gatherings. Here is an upright man or woman who respects the people and conversations around him, and assiduously avoids the most accessible temptation in today's office. Managers who believe in regular tweeting are banned from applying for this award, and those who constantly circulate or receive lewd or other jokes by SMS are unlikely to win in any case because that fleeting smile on their faces gives it all away.

The 'Good Food' Oscar

This award goes to the manager who arranges the best lunch or snacks at meetings. Aren't we fed up of those oily samosas and chips served during late evening sessions, or that greasy chicken curry and rubbery paneer butter masala served during lunch at offsite meetings? This, when there are so many wonderful, diverse and affordable food options around us. With some planning and no additional budget, our managers can ensure exotic Mexican fare or tasty chaat in the evenings, and delicious Chettinad- or Gujarati-themed cuisine for lunch. Special marks should be given to the choice of dessert while evaluating contenders for this award because a nice, light sweet dish with character rounds off an excellent office meal perfectly. Owners or contractors who run canteens in our offices are also welcome to compete for this prestigious award.

The 'Shortest Meetings' Oscar

Long, interminable meetings have become the bane of our lives. If the amount of time spent in meaningless meetings is added up, the result may entirely explain the yawning productivity gap between India and China. So, our second category is for the person who organizes the shortest meetings throughout the year. He or she can be your peer, team member or boss. All the nominee must do is ensure that every meeting is extremely short, focused only on the issue at hand and always begins and ends on time. Organizers of any meeting where doodling or sleeping or daydreaming is noticed are instantly disqualified.

The 'Item Number' Oscar

This will be the biggest Office Oscar of them all because if offices are to be interesting places, they need interesting people. If everyone was a workaholic manager like me, or an expert IT specialist or manufacturing expert focused on work alone, the office would soon resemble a graveyard without a ghost. Fortunately, our Item Number Oscar award has been specifically constituted to deal with this problem. It will be awarded to the most interesting person in office—someone who has attitude and spunk, has broken a few rigid norms, created some innocent mischief, violated a few meaningless office codes or played a few harmless tricks which have made the office come abuzz with life. Colleagues who have stoked controversies during the year are encouraged to apply. Members of senior management, mostly a sedate lot, may have to keep their distance for this one.

I hope to apply in the 'Good Food' category, but my colleagues will tell you most emphatically that I will never ever be nominated for the 'Shortest Meetings' Oscar.

33

PERM Yourself in Office

If you are an executive over forty, a programme in extreme reverse mentoring, or PERM, can be invaluable.

Mentoring is now a well-regarded practice in many good organizations. It typically involves a young executive being mentored by an older manager who provides insights and guidance. Reverse mentoring, which has also been spoken about in management literature but is not as common in Indian companies, is the opposite. It involves a senior manager being mentored by a junior or 'Gen Y' colleague, with a focus on acquiring the new-age knowledge that the young person is familiar with.

This column takes forward the nascent thinking on reverse mentoring with the idea of a 'programme of extreme reverse mentoring (PERM)', which we think can be invaluable for older Indian executives. Simply put, PERM involves a manager who is over forty (since we are polite, we won't use the term middle-aged here) being mentored by an extremely young colleague who is younger than twenty-five—either just out of college or a couple of years into a job. It also involves at least two informal hours per month when the mentor and mentee meet, preferably over an extremely nice meal hosted by the older person. Read on to consider the benefits of PERM; we hope you decide to enrol yourself in this programme.

Learn the Digital Ropes

When I wanted to understand Picasa or Twitter, I headed shamelessly to the youngest executive in our office. It worked very well for me, though I suspect the young lady was shocked that such an ignoramus could exist at the senior levels of the company. For youngsters below twenty-five or even a little older, these digital platforms are second nature. They tend to know the inner workings of WhatsApp, Instagram, Pinterest, Facebook, etc. better than you perhaps know your spouse or partner. A couple of PERM hours and you can also be an expert—though of course you predate these digital wonders by several years. Your mentor can also be your constant digital guide thereafter.

The Weekend Coach

Many forty-plus Indian managers, unlike their Western counterparts, find it difficult to disconnect from work over weekends. They are hopelessly addicted (or at the very least, constantly plugged in) to their work papers and thoughts, emails and shop-talk type of telephone conversations. On the other hand, many young executives are clear that their weekends are for family, partying, adventure or pursuing extra-curricular passions. PERM sessions can make you realize the true value of weekends and how much you are missing out on, as your mentor talks to you with great excitement about how he or she rocked the dance floor on Saturday night or went trekking with friends or jammed with a guitar or just chilled out with a sibling. You can even request their expertise to help you plan your weekend in advance, but then be prepared for the unexpected.

The Cool Hangout Guide

Older managers generally want to be purposeful and active all the time, sometimes just to feel important. Youngsters, on the other hand, know it is cool to just hang out sometimes and have fun. In addition, they can also tell you about the really cool places to hang out in your city. Oldies like me may know a few fine-dining restaurants well, but through PERM, you can discover the best streetside food spots, the coolest bars and fusion lounges, and the best spots on the road or seaside to snuggle up with your partner. I never knew about cool holiday places to visit through Airbnb until a young colleague mentioned this to me, and then she said with a smile—'So now you know whom to ask!'

Hone Your Multitasking Skills

If you think you are good at multitasking, just observe a twenty-five-year-old executive or trainee in your office on a busy workday. There are points at which they are doing a couple of quick things on their smartphone even as they simultaneously punch their computer keys with ease, talk fluently on the

telephone and casually eat their samosa or sandwich. The speed
at which they type text messages is incredible, even as they follow
up on their project or organize the next meeting. Perhaps this
wonderful capability is derived from the new-age student habit
of doing homework, being on Facebook, watching television
shows and talking on the telephone—all at the same time.
PERM can help you improve at all this multitasking stuff by
picking up valuable tips from your young mentor, both through
observation and coaching, but you have to be a serious learner.

What the Youth Really Want

We are a relatively young country, and the youth therefore
represent one of the largest consumer markets. If you are a
senior manager in a business that hopes to make inroads into the
youth segment, you need to get a pulse of what they really want.
Consumer research can help, but nothing can work better than
a few informal PERM sessions with your mentor and his or her
friends. You will learn what they value and desire, whom they
respect, the language they speak and the stuff they don't care
about. On a different but related note, some of these PERM
sessions will also tell you whether your young colleagues are
really enjoying working in your office, and, if not, why. You
may even get some advice on what you can do to make the office
an interesting and exciting place to be.

Experiment

To be truly innovative, older managers like me may have to
discard time-tested methods and experiment more often. This

can be challenging, because with age we tend to get rather set in our ways. On the other hand, young executives who are just out of college are naturally experimentative in a carefree way, because that's how most university campuses are. They generally don't like sticking to rigid rules or processes, but are curious, questioning and trying new things. PERM sessions will bring experienced managers in constant contact with these experimenting ways and can eventually end up changing their mindsets for the better.

I am well over forty and happy to confess that this article has been PERM-ed up by my reverse mentor.

34

Mathematics at Work

Equations, string theory, the law of tangents—why all these concepts are relevant for managers.

A few years ago, the announcement that two mathematicians of Indian origin, Manjul Bhargava and Subhash Khot, had won two of the most coveted international prizes in this 'queen of sciences' in a single year, made mathematics fashionable once again in our country. During that time, I even heard mathematics come up for discussion at an office party, where it amazingly took precedence over the usual assorted shoptalk and cubicle grapevine.

A common but incorrect perception is that Indian managers have little or no inclination or interest in mathematics. An even more uncharitable view is that many managers are somewhat scared of this formidable subject. But the fact is that as office workers, we engage with several mathematical concepts every day of our working lives. Don't believe this? Read on to understand how the lives of managers are constantly entwined with mathematics.

Addition

One of the simplest ideas in mathematics is the addition of two or more numbers to produce a sum or total. Managers are familiar with this concept. Every day, they witness the constant addition of work to their pending tasks, and the number of unfinished tasks thus keeps adding up, like a grand total on the move. The boss keeps adding work to one's plate, and the HR (human resource) and finance teams do their bit by giving us some chore to do. Many emails contribute to this constant addition of jobs, not to mention the phone calls from the spouse.

Subtraction

Smart managers respond to this barrage of addition by applying the idea of subtraction, yet another mathematical operation. They subtract the number of things they have to do by delegating some jobs to others, by immediately deleting tasks they consider unnecessary, and by shelving matters which are not important or urgent. If you see an executive with a clean table, you know that he is a master at subtraction.

Multiplication

Chief executive officers (CEOs) and managers learn the Corporate Theory of Multiplication quickly. This theory simply states that the number of problems or issues that any company will face will multiply with the passing of every single day, unless they are acted upon promptly. A corollary to this theory is that managers should only focus on taking the right actions to address these multiple problems, without getting unduly anxious about them. Any other approach can lead to multiplication of health and wellness issues too, which is not a desirable state for either managers or mathematicians.

Drawing Lines

Lines are at the heart of the visual branch of mathematics known as geometry. These are also at the heart of every corporate enterprise. Here, the lines which clearly matter are the top line (the revenue you generate) and the bottom line (the profits you earn). Both these lines dominate executives' lives, and eventually end up taking a toll on their hairlines and waistlines. Managers, in the meanwhile, obsess over all these lines, thus making them experts in this entire area.

Equations

Mathematics—in particular, algebra—is all about equations, with each equation trying to solve for unknown variables, generally denoted as X, Y and Z. Managers too know that workspaces and careers are all about equations with multiple people such as colleagues, superiors, team members and agency personnel. In fact, many of these same people are the unknown variables a manager tries to solve for. Also, because a good number of such people keep changing their views and motivations unpredictably, quite often corporate equations become far more challenging to resolve than the regular ones which involve X and Y. Smart managers must become adept at equations.

String Theory

There is an interesting branch of mathematics called string theory, where physical particles are replaced by one-dimensional objects called strings. In our offices, though, string theory takes a different shape. It essentially consists of various people or departments who try to string you along by putting forward various promises or assurances. It is important that managers quickly figure out the manipulators of such strings, by learning to distinguish the true from the false. Once you master string theory, no one can take you for a ride.

Law of Tangents

The law of tangents is an essential principle in mathematics, which draws a direct relationship between the tangential angles of a triangle and the length of its sides. Managers encounter an interesting version of this law, which establishes a similarly clear relationship between the tangential nature of any official discussion and its length. This states that if your boss or colleague is talking at a tangent on any subject (which we know happens quite often), then the length of the meeting is likely to be unduly extended, and no productive result will ever be achieved. Managers can solve this knotty problem by finding the simplest excuse (an important client call that cannot be postponed, perhaps) to leave such meetings.

Regression Analysis

We will not explain mathematical regression analysis in great detail here, except to say that it tries to establish a firm relationship or trend between diverse variables or numbers. The same concept applies to organizations and managers, as they try to understand why sales or quality or profits have regressed steadily over the past several months and years. Could the reason for such regression be the heavy rainfall in the factory, or people in south India brushing their teeth less often, or the slowing economy, perhaps? Many managers are experts at such regression analysis, and the causes they identify are most often totally outside their control. Such expertise unfortunately also leads to the regression of careers, because good management theory believes that managers should firmly take charge and deliver.

Laws of Probability

Probability is yet another important branch of mathematics, and one that is constantly applied in all offices. For instance, if your boss has a firm point of view which is opposed to yours, the probability that his view will eventually prevail is close to 100%. If you are launching a product or marketing campaign next week, the probability that everything is under control as of today is close to zero. If you feel like eating chicken biryani for lunch today, the probability that your office canteen will have this delicious dish on the menu is low, but you can probably head to a restaurant outside and rectify matters at a cost. Managers, like mathematicians, soon realize that some probabilities can be altered but not all. That's life.

In my opinion, an excellent mathematical concept which has given great grief to managers is the bell curve, which determines annual performance ratings and bonuses in many companies.

35

Meet Shakespeare, the Manager's Guru

Here are some powerful lessons for CEOs and managers from the greatest writer in the English language.

The world of English literature has paid some great tributes to Shakespeare, with conferences, plays, street performances and talks being organized across the world.

It is now time for businesses to pay homage to the timeless bard as well. Typically, corporate tributes are focused on people such as chairpersons, chief executive officers (CEOs) and professors of management. This piece has, therefore, taken upon itself the task of saluting Shakespeare, and pointing out that he is not just another great writer, but also one of the greatest management gurus who has ever lived.

Shakespeare's writings hold profound lessons and while there is enough material in his writings for several leadership workshops, here is a primer of some powerful lessons we can learn from him.

No One Is Indispensable

Many Indian companies build a myth of indispensability around some of their key managers. Indeed, so many of us feel we are so indispensable that we even hesitate to go on a long vacation. Shakespeare shatters this myth totally with these evocative words from *As You Like It*: 'All the world's a stage, and all the men and women merely players. They have their exits and their entrances.' We need to recognize that in the larger scheme of things, companies are also stages, and we are merely actors on these stages for a period of time. Each of us will have our entrances and exits, and the play will then go on. We will, of course, strut our stuff on our corporate stages each day, and we should do so to the best of our abilities—but we should never mistake the applause when the curtain comes down as a testament to our indispensability. For many actors can play any specific role superbly—even if these are challenging parts such as Othello or Macbeth. Shakespeare's own plays have demonstrated this truth for 450 years now.

Comic Relief Is Useful Too

Indian companies are often ultra-serious places; our conferences and meeting rooms are mostly full of grim and staid conversations. As we rise up the corporate ranks, we increasingly lose the ability to laugh at ourselves or to use occasional humour as a useful method for taking discussions forward. Yet, some of the best managers I have known use humour as a very powerful tool, to illustrate an important point, to cool tempers or to bring people together. Shakespeare teaches us that comic relief can be of much use, even in the midst of the most terrible tragedies. A good example of this is in *Macbeth*, where a drunk porter indulges in comic revelry between such terrifying events as the murder of King Duncan and the discovery of his body. This inebriated porter talks at great length about the three things that drink provokes. 'Nose-painting, sleep and urine', he says, and then goes on to add, 'Lechery, sir, it provokes and unprovokes: it provokes the desire but takes away the performance.' Whether or not we agree with his conclusions, he certainly makes us smile at a tense point in the play. Similarly, in *Hamlet*, a couple of clowns fool around in a gravedigging scene, immediately after the tragic suicide of Ophelia. These comic sequences lift the plays and ensure even sharper audience attention to the serious parts that follow. Our managers would do well to learn to laugh and smile.

Listen Before You Speak

In general, Indians tend to be poor listeners. Indian managers love speaking—primarily about themselves, their achievements and vision. These days, they also hold forth generously about their views on new-age topics such as e-commerce, gender diversity, cultural sensitivity and helping the spouse by changing nappies at home. Therefore, Shakespeare's advice to us on listening, and not speaking too much, is invaluable. 'Give thy thoughts no tongue,' he tells us in *Hamlet*. He is cautioning us here to think before we speak, to keep our thoughts to ourselves and only talk when necessary. Shakespeare goes on to say, also in *Hamlet*, 'Give every man thy ear, but few thy voice,' thus emphasizing the importance of listening to people within organizations. Unless we listen carefully to others and to those around us, how will we ever learn?

Be True to Your Own Style

There is an increasing tendency among executives to emulate their corporate idols and their methods of leadership. This has led to a rash of books about the styles of Steve Jobs, Richard Branson, Mark Zuckerberg and other highly successful businessmen. In addition, many managers also try to ape the leaders of their own companies, either because they are awestruck, or because they see this as a politically correct choice. Shakespeare warns us against such blind pursuit of the leadership styles of others, however iconic they may be. He advises us in *Hamlet*, 'This above all: to thine own self be true . . .' This is a wonderful line with deep meaning. We blossom as leaders when we are true to ourselves, in harmony with our own selves. We should consider integrating key lessons from other great leaders into our methods of management only where these are not in conflict with our own natural styles. For instance, a manager who has a deep belief in consumer research or in consulting his senior team before arriving at critical decisions, will be committing a great error in trying to follow the rather dramatic methods associated with Jobs, just because he was so successful.

Inspiration Can Move Mountains

Shakespeare's plays are replete with powerful examples of how inspiring leaders can lead their teams towards achieving the impossible. The most memorable example of this is the brilliant speech delivered by King Henry V (in the play with the same name) at the battlefield scene at Agincourt, where he rallies his tired and demoralized English troops against the might of a much larger, highly armoured and skilled French army. Every corporate leader should read and imbibe this stirring address, because it remains to this day the finest dramatic interpretation of what inspiring leadership means, even under the most adverse circumstances. Here are just a few lines from *Henry V* to whet your appetite: 'From this day to the ending of the world, but we in it shall be remembered, we few, we happy few, we band of brothers, for he today that sheds his blood with me, shall be my brother; and gentlemen in England now abed, shall think themselves accursed they were not here, and hold their manhoods cheap whiles any speaks, that fought with us upon Saint Crispin's Day.'

The English soldiers, thus roused by their magnificent leader, went on to win the battle against impossible odds.

The simple message from Shakespeare: Leaders have to inspire their teams, particularly when the chips are down.

I think that the best lesson corporate managers can learn from Shakespeare is contained in this quote from Richard II: *'The purest treasure mortal times afford is spotless reputation. That away, men are but gilded loam or painted clay.'*

36

Become a JEDI

To be happy and successful at work, follow the 'Just Excel, Don't Impress' (JEDI) code.

The bruising nature of some workplaces has been highlighted by a well-circulated article on Amazon's office culture. This piece, originally published in the *New York Times* some years ago, claims that employees in Amazon are encouraged to work at an unrelenting pace and to literally 'climb the wall' when they hit one. We don't know how true these claims are, but we do know, deep within our hearts, that our workplaces can be both nurturing and bruising. And one way we bruise ourselves badly in the workplace is by trying to impress others.

Many of us are constantly trying to dazzle bosses, colleagues and team members. We often speak up only to wow others, make glitzy presentations to impress them, and sometimes even dress up to impress our colleagues. Trying to impress so many people constantly is exhausting. Often, it simply does not work, which adds to our frustration. Sometimes it may even backfire, if the person you are trying to impress thinks you are overdoing it. And, most importantly, it may take the focus away from doing excellent work, which is what finally counts. This piece will tell you how to be a new JEDI—Just Excel, Don't Impress—at work. May the force be with you.

Speak Only When You Need To

In meetings where the boss is present, we often try to speak up to impress. There is an overarching feeling in some offices that sheer participation in such sessions is essential to making your presence felt. This is incorrect, because a good boss sees through such 'participation' very quickly. In addition, driven by your urge to speak, you often end up saying something silly or contributing little genuine content. So don't speak at meetings to impress others—it is tiresome and nerve-wracking for you. Speak only when you have something new to say, a fresh perspective to add to what has already been said, or when you have a genuinely new thought to contribute. Spend the rest of the time listening. Listening helps you to reflect on what is being discussed with an open mind. It helps you generate new thoughts and ideas for your work. The urge to speak and impress others sometimes shuts out the openness to listen.

Focus on Content

In our desire to impress, we spend huge amounts of time in creating slick PowerPoint presentations, great-looking reports, and many similar types of output. Think about this deeply for a moment, and you will immediately see how wasteful this method of trying to make an impression is. Lots of colourful, animated graphs, charts and pictures, tucked away in hundreds of slides, do not really constitute meaningful content. In many cases, these trappings tend to distract from what you are really trying to say, and don't yield the required discussions and result. Instead, if you wish to excel and deliver a constructive presentation or report, make your points very simply. Use five slides instead of a hundred. Anything that is important can be said in a simple line or two, or through a few key data points, so don't waste your time on all the fluff. Instead, say these two lines as powerfully as you can. That is most likely to produce results, and it will also conserve your energy.

Be a Team Player

We try to constantly impress others when we are overly caught up with ourselves as individuals, and our own desire to individually stand out. On the other hand, when we focus on contributing to the overall success of our team, we prioritize excellence in content—on doing what each of us is assigned to do, in the best possible manner. Eventually, in most professional organizations, individuals win only when the team wins. So, clearly, being a great team player is the best approach, and one that has the potential to create the most win-win situations for everyone. This team approach also takes away the pressure of trying to impress others, an endeavour which always ends up dissipating a lot of valuable personal energy.

Work Smart, Don't Stay Late

We often want to prove to our bosses and colleagues that we are always working hard, because there is always so much to be done. Staying late in the office simply because others are doing so is not an indicator of hard work. By doing so, we want people to think that we are willing to sacrifice our precious personal lives (that is, if we have any) to contribute to the noble corporate cause. This is nonsense, because hardly anything meaningful is achieved by staying on at work late into the evening. In addition, you end up eating assorted late-evening snacks, which will further impact your waistline. Our advice: Work smart throughout the day. Scrupulously avoid digital distractions during office hours, because these can suck up an amazing amount of time. Focus relentlessly on the most important priority jobs, and on completing them well. Then, pack up and go home (or for a session with friends or at the gym) at a predetermined hour. Check out how happy this makes you feel.

I think that we often make the best impression when we don't try to impress.

37

Einstein on the Job

Navigating black holes and other lessons that office-goers can learn from the Theory of Relativity.

In the early twentieth century, Albert Einstein announced to the world his Theory of Relativity. This theory shook the world of physics and has since then transformed our entire understanding of the universe. Fundamentally, the theory fused the three dimensions of space with the dimension of time, to create a four-dimensional world where many strange things could happen, and only the speed of light remained fixed.

However, it is said that very few people have truly understood the Theory of Relativity and all its implications, as it involves complex science and serious thinking. It is unlikely that many people will understand it in the near future either because complexity and deep thinking do not go too well with the modern mind, which is either weighed down by a thousand thoughts, or at other times, blissfully chilled out. On the other hand, office-goers can gain significantly from understanding a few simple aspects of Einstein's theory. So, to pay tribute to this theory which is now well over a hundred years old, I present below an elementary and somewhat irreverent guide to Einstein, relativity and the office.

A Second and an Hour

When Einstein was asked to describe his magnificent theory in simple words, he famously said: 'When you are courting a nice girl, an hour seems like a second. When you sit on a red-hot cinder, a second seems like an hour. That is relativity.' Now, all of us working in modern offices know this feeling. When we are discussing an exciting, practical business model or marketing an idea across the table, an hour does seem to fly by. On the other hand, when we are sitting in a conference room, listening to a long-winded PowerPoint presentation, a second seems like an eternity. That's office relativity for you. Drop all those PowerPoint slides and meaningless diagrams and get to the essence of what you want to say. That will get you relatively far greater attention and interest, from everyone around.

Black Holes

One of the predictions of the Theory of Relativity is the existence of black holes in the universe. Simply put, these are deep holes from which nothing can escape, not even a glimmer of light. In arriving at this prediction, Einstein's theory has put its finger on something that is very relevant to modern office life—they contain numerous black holes. When emails are sent to these black holes, there is generally no response. When project reports are submitted to them, the black holes never revert with any views or approval. When you deal with such black holes, there is often no escape because they have tied you up in meaningless questions and knots, mostly because they are unclear about what to do. Just like spaceships should avoid black holes in the universe, we suggest that office-goers do their best to avoid black holes in our offices.

Time Travellers

Einstein's Theory of Relativity makes it theoretically possible for human beings to travel backwards in time. However, scientists are still searching for actual evidence of such time travel. We would like to proudly inform everyone that lots of evidence for travelling backwards in time can be found in our offices.

Whenever a new boss joins, he travels back in time constantly to prove that mostly everything his predecessor has done is wrong and needs to be changed. Whenever older managers such as myself want to prove a point in the midst of a heated discussion, we like to travel back in time and say—'I did this ten years ago and it worked beautifully. So, tell me why it will not work now.' Youngsters who were not in the company a decade ago, or even till recently, are then effectively silenced, unless they can think like Einstein and come up with an immediate counter-response. Many companies and senior executives like to dwell at length on the glorious achievements of their past.

Now, all this takes attention away from the future, which is the direction of time travel that we should encourage if our teams are to focus on what needs to be done and succeed. So, whenever you notice backward time travel, here's a suggestion: Do your best to quickly move the needle towards the future.

Expanding Universe

Yet another result derived from the Theory of Relativity is that the universe is constantly expanding, and the far boundaries are moving away from us. This is exactly the case with most organizations. Executives are happy to come up with a constantly expanding universe of ideas—new things to do, new acquisitions to consider, new sub-brands to launch, new assets to invest in, new roles to fill. Unfortunately, this constantly expanding universe often takes away the focus from core areas, and from executing the most important things to win in our industries.

To stop the endless expansion of this universe, it is important for all of us who lead teams to relentlessly and objectively review new ideas, and only permit those ideas that are essential for progress or will enable our companies to take a big leap forward. All the other ideas deserve to be trashed before they suck away time and energy without achieving anything significant.

Space to Think

It took several years for Einstein to think through and develop the Theory of Relativity. He did this by providing himself lots of space and time to think, even while he was involved in many other routine roles, such as the mundane task of evaluating patent applications in a government office. We may not have the exceptional intelligence of Einstein, but this lesson in thinking is worth its weight in gold for just about everyone.

If you wish to develop excellent, breakthrough ideas for your team and organization, give yourself adequate space and time to think. Managers are often so addicted to action that there is never time to think. This is a huge disservice to yourself. As we salute the most famous theory in modern science, let's resolve to put on our thinking caps in office as often as possible.

Einstein famously said that only two things are infinite—the universe and human stupidity, and even he was never really sure of the former.

38

What to Wear, When

Invisible cloaks, blingy sherwanis, trendy ties—how to
understand the unstated dress codes at work.

Dress codes for corporate events can be confusing. To be fair,
some codes, such as 'business suit' and 'black tie', are clear in
what they require of us. But do we really know what to wear
when we receive an invite that specifies 'urban chic' or 'semi-
formal' or 'Bollywood style' as the dress code?

A couple of weeks ago, I was invited to a 'smart casual'
party in Mumbai. I went there dressed in well-ironed khakis
and my smart navy-blue jacket, which I thought conformed
to this global ensemble requirement—even though, I must
admit, the jacket did not feel quite right for the city's
sweltering summer. At the party, I found people walking
around in jeans and light T-shirts; there were even a couple of
youngsters in hip yoga pants. I felt terribly overdressed, very
hot, and walked around awkwardly with a glass of lemonade.
Now I know I will never know where to start dressing for a
'Bollywood style' event.

There is a real need to develop communication around corporate dress codes that is practical and clear. We can help matters along by mentioning these codes in invitations or emails that we send out for our office meetings, conferences, get-togethers and similar events. Though by no means comprehensive, here are some illustrations of how to define dress codes.

Arctic Chill

The 'Arctic Chill' dress code is recommended for all offices and conference rooms where erratic air-conditioning creates a freezer-like environment from time to time. We see participants shivering in such hostile climatic conditions, but unable to express themselves because no one really knows whom to speak to or what to do. As a last resort in such circumstances, the air-conditioning gets brutally switched off by someone, and then the room warms up immediately like a sauna. So the Arctic Chill dress code is simple—it involves bringing along a thick sweater or pullover that can be worn or removed at short notice, based on air-conditioning performance.

Totally Casual

This dress code removes, in one single stroke, any ambiguity inherent in codes such as smart casual, business casual and semi-casual. Indian executives are known to interpret these phrases in their own rather casual ways. 'Totally casual' solves this problem, because it clarifies that the dress is entirely flexible and as casual as you want it to be. You can wear jeans, T-shirts,

skirts, yoga pants, chinos, beach shirts, shorts, sandals—
anything that is decent to wear is permissible. A nice variant of
this code could be 'Totally casual and colourful', but then you
stand the risk of loud neon colour excesses that are trending
everywhere these days.

Jacket and Tie

Here is the simplest way to describe business semi-formal dress,
which we expect men to wear to most office receptions and
business events. And if a tie is not essential, then this can be
easily modified to 'Jacket without Tie', which you will agree is
easily understood. If you want the event to wear a somewhat
colourful air, you can try 'Jacket and Cool Tie'. I have two such
cool ties, one featuring Winnie the Pooh and the other with a
picture of James Bond with a smoking gun in his right hand,
and I am waiting to wear them when I receive such an invite. I
recognize the need to evolve an equivalent, simple terminology
for business dress for women, but would like to leave this happy
task to a more knowledgeable woman reader.

Shabby Chic

Here is an invitation to wear clothing that appears somewhat
crumpled and uncared for, yet is stylish and cool. Any modern or
ethnic attire is encouraged as long as it looks somewhat shabby.
This is ideal for pretentious events that bring together corporate
types who are keen on the arts, including literature and theatre
festivals, or evenings with musicians and poets. Faded bush-
shirts, shapeless kurtas, half-creased linen pants, baggy clothes

that look half a century old, overgrown stubble—all this is encouraged, because the underlying theme is that if you aspire to be a creative kind of guy—even if you are not—you have the license to be shabby and unkempt.

Desi Festive

In India, we are fortunate to have several festival days in a year, given the cosmopolitan nature of most of our offices. Between Diwali, Easter, Eid, Pongal, Baisakhi, Ugadi, Navroz, Navaratri, Onam and so on, there are at least thirty days a year that all of us can rightfully celebrate in style. Our offices should leverage this great bounty of festivals. For all these special days, a wonderful dress code to recommend to colleagues is 'Desi Festive', which includes sherwanis, silk sarees, dhotis, bandhgalas . . . in short, whatever is the authentic style of the specific festival or region. Initial research has shown that this festive dress code has the potential to significantly perk up office happiness, can lead to more spontaneous creativity at work, and of course to a million joyous postings on Facebook and Instagram.

Invisible Cloak

There are some meetings—such as tough quarterly reviews conducted by the CEO himself, or crisis sessions where urgent and onerous work responsibilities are being allocated—where many of us would prefer to remain relatively unseen by the boss. The right dress code for these meetings is a cloak which provides invisibility, but since only magicians like Harry Potter possess this, the closest equivalent is a white or pale blue shirt with a small collar, which merges totally into the upholstery. Bright colours and big, bold checks must be avoided at all costs. Of course, as a responsible employee, I don't recommend that any executive shirk responsibility, but I know that there are some days when you need to be inconspicuous, and your dress can help you.

My all-time favourite dress code for summer is colourful shorts and a loose cotton shirt on a beachside in Goa.

39

For Your Next Offsite, Opt for Offbeat Destinations

Interesting and unusual venues that can lead to productive and happy meetings.

Recently, the company that I work for organized an offsite conference in Amritsar. This was a big departure from the common offsite locations that many companies tend to head to—Goa, Phuket or the five-star hotel down the road. Amritsar was a refreshing change. Apart from a very productive conference, and some delightful Punjabi food (Amritsari chole are heavenly), many participants made time to visit places that only a few people had seen before—the Golden Temple, Jallianwala Bagh, Wagah Border and the evocative Partition Museum.

Whether you have a big budget (unlikely) or a small one (more likely), there are many unusual places you can choose for your organization's next offsite. Here is a possible list.

University Campuses

For offsites that involve engaged sessions, such as case studies or lectures, universities and business school campuses are good options, and cost-effective too. They have the required teaching infrastructure and, for many managers, a return to the classroom subliminally signals new learning. The mind opens up when seated in classrooms, I think, rather than at a glitzy hotel. University campuses generate a happy sense of student nostalgia, particularly when you sit at the chaiwallah's shop after the day's work is done.

Museums

If you are planning a conference where some sharp, insightful thinking is required, museums are great venues. Many museums have conference halls and large lawns adjoining them. By their very nature, museums encourage curation of the best thoughts and wonderful storytelling. And a conducted tour of the exhibits can provide participants an intellectual voyage that few other places can.

The High Seas

A conference on board a ship is an interesting idea. Ships are not so accessible or affordable, though, so some extra planning will be required. But a conference that also doubles up as a cruise certainly has a romantic flavour to it. I also think the vastness of the sea induces a sense of calm and therefore makes for far more congenial conferences, particularly if there are contentious topics on the agenda.

Towns with Themes

There are many towns in India which are generally not high up on the conference map, but can make for excellent offsite locations because they have such interesting themes. For instance, Amritsar is about the Sikh religion, the Independence struggle and Partition. Similarly, Munnar is about tea plantations and, of course, sheer natural beauty. Think of Visakhapatnam, Mysuru, Madurai, Udaipur, Guwahati, Kochi or Leh. All towns with wonderful themes.

Theatres

If your offsite conference requires lots of space and dollops of creative thinking, your local theatre is a good place to consider. Theatres are generally perceived as creative hubs: they have the required seating capacity and also a large dais for speakers. To make the conference memorable, you could consider adding a play by a local theatre group to the agenda or even encourage participants to stage a play themselves, which is fun and also encourages teamwork.

Ashrams and Yoga Centres

For offsites where a key objective is to relax and recharge, ashrams and yoga centres can potentially deliver the goods. If you have the budget, you could choose Rishikesh or elsewhere in the Himalayas. Otherwise there are good ashrams on the periphery of many cities, with meeting room facilities as well. Here, a conference packaged along with a yoga programme could be a bonus. An added advantage is sattvic vegetarian food and a no-alcohol rule, which may enable everyone to detoxify themselves and, with some luck, also lose a kilo or two.

A Corporate Campus (Not Your Own, Silly)

An offsite conference at the campus of another corporate firm that is not your competitor is an interesting idea. Many corporates have large and interesting campuses today, equipped with conference centres. Typically, these are located in city suburbs, or in IT parks. An added bonus can be a learning mission to that organization's facilities. Taking forward this idea needs some networking and may also require you to offer a reciprocal arrangement to the other organization.

Back to Goa

If every other option fails, there is always Goa. We love going back there for offsites of all hues. Goa has the beaches, affordable wine (important) and bohemian air that make for a perfect combination. Every time I land in Goa for an offsite, I smell the totally relaxed, salty air and fall in love with the place all over again.

I think every offsite requires a great disc jockey, because there is nothing like some inspired dancing to round up a great conference.

40

The Art of ACE-ing Your Office Conversations

In this age of distractions, how do you ensure unwavering attention to your colleagues?

If there is one habit many office workers can benefit from in the New Year, it is giving others the gift of attention. We are constantly distracted at our workplaces today—telephone calls, WhatsApp messages, emails, social media, open office chatter, constant interruptions, and cricket scores. This has resulted in a worrying lack of attention, leading to frustratingly disengaged conversations.

The remedy is simple: Aim to ACE (Attentive Conversations Every time) whenever you talk with colleagues. The rules of ACE are simple—pay attention to what the person in front of you is saying and ensure that you speak mindfully and attentively. What we need to master are the methods of this important art form. Here is an ACE primer.

Keep That Smartphone Away

Every time you get into a meeting, keep your smartphone on the farthest table or surface in the room, far, far away from your reach. One of my colleagues does this all the time, and he tells me that this move is an absolute gamechanger, because its benefits are enormous and immediate—you no longer have to fight that temptation of reaching out to your phone every second to check on momentous new messages or mindlessly surf social media. Consequently, your total focus is on the conversation. And that works wonders for a meaningful dialogue.

Get Out of Office

Often, if you want to engage in a deep conversation without distraction, it may be best to leave the office and hop across to a nearby café. This removes you from the noise of the workplace, and there is no interruption from pesky colleagues. Just the two or three of you, with a cup of tea or coffee to liven up your senses, is a perfect setting for an excellent meeting, particularly if the topic requires your undivided attention. This works equally well for creative meetings which benefit from relaxed attention and an informal setting.

Lunchtime Walk the Talk

Never underestimate the power of walking and talking together, particularly after a good lunch. Conversations over lunchtime walks, in the roads around your office block or in a nearby park often yield attentive behaviour. The sheer rhythm of the walk helps, and if this becomes a daily or weekly ritual, then both people involved happily set aside this time exclusively for speaking with each other. In fact, this becomes a talking routine to look forward to, and is best suited for informal dialogues with close colleagues on your team on wide ranging areas of common interest.

Take Note

You can ACE a meeting by bringing your notebook along, carrying all the points you wish to discuss. These points help you track the meeting and cover ground. Further, when you develop a habit of taking down brief notes of key messages that the person in front of you is communicating, this ensures that you are attentive and constantly listening. Arriving with notes, and then taking down notes during the meeting, conveys your seriousness about the conversation, which in itself can lead to enhanced attentiveness.

Fly and Speak

An excellent ACE technique is to schedule a meeting while flying together. Book your seats next to each other on a flight and use the couple of hours en route to complete an important conversation. I can tell you from experience that this works brilliantly—no mobile signals, no intrusions (except the in-flight snacks service). What also helps is that the economy class seats are so cramped these days that it is difficult to get up frequently, so both people have no option but to sit tight and listen to each other, at close quarters. So, well before you land, you have landed all the right messages with each other.

Buffer and Focus

Quite often, we rush out of one meeting into the next. This does not bode well for attentiveness, because we carry with us raw thoughts, open questions and sometimes heightened emotions, from the first meeting that has just concluded. These take away our attention from the new meeting which we have just entered. To deal with this, do your best to provide a buffer time of at least half an hour between consecutive meetings—use this buffer to have a cup of tea, recover substantially from the first session, and enter the second discussion with a clear, attentive mind. Buffering takes some effort, because you may have to convince others to move meeting schedules around a bit—but it is an ACE habit.

Short Is Sweet

An ACE trick up your sleeve (that's where your wristwatch normally is) is to define a tight duration for each conversation. Both people then know, right from the start, that time is short and the agenda at hand has to be concluded quickly, so they tend to remain very attentive and focused throughout the meeting. If the default time slot you normally use for a meeting is sixty minutes, try reducing it to thirty. Shorter time slots work really well for transactional and routine meetings. And as you become increasingly better at short conversations, you can gift time back to your colleague and yourself, by finishing early. Everyone welcomes the gift of time.

My ACE habit is to make and keep eye contact with the person I am having a conversation with because I believe that the eyes are windows to the mind.

41

SOAR above the Job

Learn how to Switch Off and Recharge (SOAR) after office hours if you want to stay energized at work.

The most productive, energetic and happy managers I know find ways of seamlessly switching off from work after a productive day in the office. Conversely, people who constantly find work-related thoughts intruding into their leisure time find themselves becoming increasingly anxious, fatigued and, therefore, less effective. This is especially true in today's digital age, where office workers are constantly tethered to their mobile phones, only an email away from their next point of stress.

We have all been taught how to work well, but who will teach us how to unwind equally well, so that we can begin the next day fully recharged once again? Empirical evidence shows that you are unlikely to find your guru of switching-off if you search in conventional places such as your boss, or your business school professor, or your neighbourhood human resource manager. All of them will have lots of advice for you on how to work smart and exceed your targets. But if you are really smart, you must also learn to SOAR—switch off and recharge. This column takes great pleasure in introducing you to some key tenets of the SOAR principle.

Empty Your Brain

A very effective method of switching off is to empty your brain just before you leave the office. You can achieve this by spending a few minutes at the end of each day to plan how and when to complete pending tasks. Professor Brandon Smit of Ball State University, Indiana, who has researched this interesting area, says this simple method tricks your brain into thinking that these tasks have been completed. This perhaps happens because your brain is now reassured that you have a well-thought-out action plan to resolve the incomplete tasks, and therefore feels liberated until the next day. So, empty your brain into a small end-of-day plan, and then switch off with ease.

Commute with a Friend

Use your commute at the end of the day to speak to a friend. Whether you travel by train, bus or car, phone a friend who is not from your workplace, and talk about a couple of your common interests in life. Food, sports, girlfriends or boyfriends, movies, a funny piece of news, weekend plans, friendly gossip . . . there are so many interesting, even salacious, things that your friend and you can share happily over the mobile phone, which are not rooted in our workplaces. By doing this, you will also be temporarily transforming the mobile phone from an official work device to a friendly personal accessory. From personal experience, I can tell you that talking on the phone to a friend while commuting works brilliantly and helps me switch off from work almost completely by the time I reach home.

Create a Physical Buffer

Any physical activity after a long day at work provides an excellent buffer zone where switching off from work happens gradually but surely. For those of us fortunate to live in cities where we can cycle to work, the process of cycling itself achieves this objective. A brief, intense evening workout in your gymnasium, or a nice, brisk late evening walk with your partner, has the same switch-off effect. I have no doubt your imagination will conjure up other equally interesting formats of physical buffer activity, so who am I to define the limits of physical activity that humans can engage in? The point is, you can SOAR any way you wish to.

Talk to a Familiar Stranger

An excellent way of switching off, even in the midst of a stressful day, is to talk to a familiar stranger, in or around your office. This could be the liftman, the catering boy, the receptionist, an executive in a totally different team who has nothing to do with your work, or even the paanwala or newspaper vendor who sits just outside your office. They have all the comfort of familiarity with you, yet they are relative strangers to your workplace. Talk to them about inane topics, including what they have eaten for lunch, or the popular colours that lift-commuters wear, or the low points of last week's cricket match, or why pigs have wings.

SOARing in this manner, even for a brief while, is very helpful and relaxing.

Get Yourself a Hobby

A hobby that you immerse yourself in is an excellent way of SOARing. This could be running, music, photography, bird-watching, cooking or yoga. An ideal hobby to help you relax and unwind is one that you can engage in regularly, whether it be daily or every other weekend. Hobbies also help you plan your weekend wonderfully, and well in advance. Having an uneventful, boring weekend often leads to two miserable days when your mind will wander back to the unresolved stresses and tensions of your workplace. Cultivating a hobby requires both inclination and discipline, until it eventually becomes a positive addiction that is integral to your life. You long for it, and the possibility of engaging in it during the weekend creates positive expectations throughout the week. This way, you SOAR throughout the week too.

Disengage Digitally

This is way easier said than done, but the best way of switching off in today's hyper-digital age is to be extremely disciplined with your digital devices. Some countries in Europe have mandated times beyond which official emails cannot be sent or read, but here in India, we send emails whenever we please. A practical solution is to fix an hour at night after which you won't check your mail. For me, this is 10 p.m. You could also agree with your partner that the bedroom is off-limits for digital surfing. I am yet to succeed at this but hope to make a breakthrough soon. Similarly, wake up to a nice cup of coffee and your morning newspaper before rushing for your email or social media feed. Do not become a slave to your mobile phone, because it will never let you switch off. Over weekends, if at all you need to check your email for anything urgent, do so only for a few minutes and then put it out of your mind. This is a tough ask, but if you wish to SOAR, you have to bite the digital bullet.

I SOAR when I write, which I do assiduously over the weekends.

42

Time to Think

Presentations, meetings, target-setting—the daily grind of managers can be taxing and counterproductive.

Managers just don't have time to think. Caught in an endless whirl of meetings, presentations, targets and travel, the one thing that gets squeezed out completely is thinking time. There are, of course, a couple of glorified thinking sessions each year, such as annual strategy off-sites, which provide some respite. But even these sessions are full of fancy strategy frameworks and starchy group work, all of which eventually constrain free-ranging thought.

Curiously, many of us in the corporate world also avoid deep thinking because this appears to be difficult work. It is far easier to focus on linear, familiar activities such as chasing monthly sales targets and participating in busy review meetings. And, of course, the easiest and laziest way out is to outsource thinking to consultants, many of whom then think as they think you want them to think.

In the absence of a good management training programme that teaches us how to think well, we put on our thinking cap to bring you a primer of how you can create thinking time for yourself. Give these simple suggestions some thought.

Early Bird Gets the Thought

Arrive at work half an hour early every day. Do not switch on your computer and begin responding to emails right away because this will hijack your mind. Instead, pick up a hot cup of coffee or tea; the caffeine stimulates the mind. Sit back in your chair and think about one significant opportunity or issue facing your business or team. Jot down your thoughts in a notebook, or, if you are digitally inclined, on your tablet. Think carefully and write down the pros and cons of each course of action. Stop when you wish to and continue the next morning. At the end of this session, reward yourself with another hot beverage. Now, invigorated by your thoughts, embark on your daily routine.

Commute with Your Mind

Whether you commute to office by train, bus or taxi, or whether you are chauffeured in your car, commuting time is invaluable thinking time. Think of your seat as a thought cocoon, far from the regular grind. When you are on the move, your mind has the license to wander. Use this time to read something relevant that can trigger your thinking in ways that you cannot always imagine. Look out of the window at the world passing by. I find this creates a very relaxing canvas for big-picture thinking. Use the commute occasionally to call someone whose advice you value.

Immense Value of Useless Meetings

All of us know that some meetings in office are totally useless. Yet, we are compelled to attend them either out of protocol, or because our team has to be represented, or because the big boss expects us to be there. During such meetings, sit in the last row or in a back seat. Take your notebook with you. Use this time to think about any subject that is important to you and write down your thoughts. Let others think that you are taking active notes from the meeting; this can win you some brownie points for diligence as well.

Get Yourself a Thought Partner

Sometimes the best thoughts emerge through informal discussion and debate. Not the formal strategy sessions involving a large team, just intense conversation with a couple of colleagues, on the subject at hand. This can happen if you develop a 'thought partner' in your team or office, someone with whom you can spar intellectually, who can challenge your ideas and also add to them. Have lunch at least once a week with your thought colleague and try to pick an interesting conversationalist and thinker as your partner. It also helps to have a partner who has a different background or training yet is a member of the team to which you belong—that helps bring common knowledge and uncommon perspective. Most important, however, is the chemistry of free-flowing professional conversation. That's what makes the magic and the thoughts come alive.

Half a Day to Think

If you can, leave half a day of each week free of all meetings. Typically, a Friday afternoon or a Saturday morning works best. This is easier said than done because it requires discipline, as well as some serious cooperation from your colleagues. Use this time to read something you have always wanted to catch up on or drop into the offices of a few interesting colleagues who generally have a point of view. Or visit the neighbourhood cafe and ruminate over a cup of coffee on the week that has gone by and some areas of work that need revisiting. For some people, the pleasant chatter in a coffee shop can trigger their own thinking.

Walk, Cycle or Run

Great thinkers and poets have waxed eloquent about the stimulating effect of a solitary walk through the forest or by the seaside. Many leaders use similar walks or runs to come to difficult decisions which require intense thought. This can work for all of us too. Find a nice park in your city to walk or jog in. Cycle to work, if your town permits you this luxury. I find cycling on the roads of Mumbai impossible and life-threatening, but stationary cycling at my gymnasium gives me similar time to think. And, of course, once in a while, put on your sneakers and head out for a walk on the nearby hills or seaside.

Learn to Say No

If you have to create valuable thinking time for yourself, you have to learn to say no to the zillion requests for meetings and conferences that reach you, and which are not truly important. Ask yourself: is this meeting essential or incredibly useful to my life and career? Let your answer speak for itself and, over time, the rest of the world will know and accept you as this kind of person. Not an easy course of action to pursue, but one that will yield wonderful results. When you say no to the superfluous, you say yes to thinking.

I have discovered that my best thinking time is when I sit down to write. So, I write every Sunday morning and then celebrate with chilled beer at lunchtime, which stimulates my thinking too.

43

What Your Cubicle Says about You

Office workers can be segmented into various types based on a study of our workspaces.

Your colleagues and you may sit in the same office, with the same overall decor, but if you reflect for a moment, every cubicle is really quite different. You only have to peek into a few cubicles, or cast your eye over a few worktables, to realize that this difference can be vast. However, a few clear patterns do emerge—some cubicles are neat and tidy, and some others in a state of eternal tumult. Some workspaces are particularly nice and warm, others cold and clinical.

I believe that office workers like ourselves can actually be segmented into various types, based on a study of our cubicles. This can help address the needs of each segment with greater care. Our human resources teams should undertake insightful studies such as this. But because they don't, I bring you a primer on Workspace-Inspired Segmentation of Employees (which folds into a nice acronym, WISE). Here are some important WISE segments.

Extremely Minimalist

The extremely minimalist cubicle is very neat and clean, with not a single paper on the table, the softboards rather bare and absolutely nothing out of place. In fact, you may mistake this cabin for one that is unoccupied, until you see a colleague sitting there. Note carefully how rapidly this colleague deals with papers that reach him or her, writing something on each of them immediately, and then despatching them off the table with great speed. If you leave anything behind in these cubicles, even with good intent, you will never see it again, because your colleague is bound to dispose of it immediately. I suspect many of these extremely minimalist people are obsessed with cleanliness, but to their genuine credit, they also reduce the workload of the cleaning staff. A final point: this segment of meticulous managers has become quite rare, so there should be an office guideline protecting them before they go extinct.

Happy Mountaineer

The happy mountaineer firmly believes in mountains of paper everywhere. You will see huge piles of paper and documents on his table, on the side racks, often on the floors as well. These mountains grow bigger each day. You may think this person will never find a required paper within this hilly mess, but this is precisely where you would be mistaken—because many happy mountaineers know exactly where to search for a particular document, and they will dive right in with great accuracy. Unfortunately, this knowledge is confined only to the occupant of the cubicle, and should you want to find something in his or her absence, banish the thought because that is virtually impossible. Once in a few years, the happy mountaineer will attempt a grand cleaning up, and during this operation, the office will resemble a combination of an earthquake-stricken area and a battlefield. During such moments, please leave the happy mountaineer alone.

Family and Friends

The 'family and friends' person is determined to demonstrate to everyone in office his or her expansive and impressive personal network. This cubicle is, therefore, marked by warm and fuzzy photographs of the spouse and self, children, parents, sometimes even grandparents, and occasionally the parents-in-law as well. Then on the softboards you will find photographs and picture postcards of friends and self on holidays to Europe or Japan, treks in some other exotic land, people smiling at the camera in the midst of fancy restaurant meals, or holding big frothy pitchers of beer at a bar—you get the picture. Even the coffee mug used here may have a family or friends' picture printed on it. You may be left wondering whether this is a cubicle or a memorabilia store, but as long as your colleague feels at home in this family environment, and does his or her work brilliantly, well, this is all to good effect.

Great Achiever

The great achiever's cubicle or office is unmistakably glorious. To begin with, there is a line-up of awards or trophies that the person has won over the years, all polished and shining. Then there are certificates that line the walls or softboards—rows of certificates that reveal the remarkable extent and scale of achievement in many diverse spheres. These could be certificates from universities, industry bodies, bosses, executive education programmes, sales conferences and so forth. Don't go too close to read them because they are meant to generally impress at a distance, and may even contain a couple of certificates from high-school painting contests.

Finally, there are photographs that show the great achiever receiving various awards from celebrities and public figures, as indisputable proof of the wonderful achievements on display. Nothing pleases the Great Achiever more than yet another award or certificate to line his walls, which is an insight the organization can usefully bear in mind.

The Intellectual

The intellectual's workspace is, first and foremost, marked by an impressive line-up of books. You will find here books on management, economics, history, accounting, finance, law, biographies—not to mention arcane fields like archaeology or quantum physics, which also occasionally make an appearance, to remind you of the high intellectual orbit which this manager operates in. These books will take the average person many lifetimes to read, but the intellectual manager has, of course, read all of them. If the books look new and unopened, don't mention this, because such a comment can have detrimental consequences for your relationship with this sort of manager. These offices also feature picture frames that contain intelligent quotations from the likes of Adam Smith, Peter Drucker, Albert

Einstein, Immanuel Kant and names you may never have heard of. Gaze at them with awe and enter and leave such offices silently and most respectfully.

This is not a comprehensive list. You may have come across many other interesting WISE segments. Please do add them here.

I belong to the WISE eaters' segment, and so my office desk always contains a few packs of healthy dark chocolate, almonds and walnuts.

44

Horseplay at Work

Here is what managers can learn from the fascinating world of horses.

Each Chinese year is named after an interesting animal, and 2014 was the year of the horse. Coming on the heels of the years of the dragon and the snake, the horse, you will agree, is a big change. Astrologers gleefully predicted a year that would gallop ahead, full of unexpected adventure, fabulous romance and great travel. Regardless of whether all this exciting stuff actually happened to you way back in 2014, here is what we can learn from horses.

Power in Office

The horse is the most energetic sign in Chinese astrology, and people born to this sign are known to be strong-minded. Truly, horses are among the most energetic of animals; there is no better symbol of fluent energy than a horse in full gallop. Perhaps that is why horsepower is an important measure of power and energy. Equally important, the horse is able to bring energy to the fore whenever required—sometimes for a Derby championship race, at other times for horse-riding with a schoolgirl in the saddle, or even as a wild horse running through vast grasslands with its mane flowing behind. Such energy is core to the animal's success. Horses thus teach managers the importance of energy at the workplace, every single day. Without consistent horsepower, very little can be achieved in your cubicle or conference room.

Vary Your Speed

Horses are masters at regulating their speed, based on circumstances or need. They can gallop at over 40 km per hour (kmph) or can canter at 20 kmph or trot at 15 kmph or also walk very slowly, at 4 kmph. They can change their pace seamlessly and, in doing so, ensure that they expend the right amount of energy for that particular phase of their journey. Managers need to learn this important lesson from the horse, and vary their pace according to the situation. If we try to gallop the whole distance, we risk a quick burnout. Yet if we only trot all the time, we will, most likely, never get ahead. Hence managers who vary their pace based on workplace needs will, in all likelihood, build successful careers for themselves.

Stick to Your Core

Some racehorses are best suited to wet courses; other horses do best on dry tracks. Hence the popular expression, 'Horses for courses'. This is equally relevant to all of us in the corporate world. Each of us has different skills, and we should focus on what we can do best.

Unfortunately, a large proportion of managers focus on roles that can help them climb the corporate ladder or jobs that are perceived to be larger or more important. For instance, I have known excellent marketers, seized with a passion for consumer behaviour or advertising, become poor profit centre heads.

This is self-destructive and, as any horse trainer can tell us, can only result in dissatisfaction everywhere. Managers need to remember that each of us is suited to a particular racecourse, and if we focus on jobs that we really like doing, which are aligned to our core skills and aptitude, it is far more likely that we will truly win in our careers.

Cover a Large Territory

Horse lovers will tell you two truths about their beloved animal. First, horses love covering large amounts of territory, and display a natural boldness in doing so. Second, these animals have an innate curiosity to check out the unusual, and don't flee from something that is merely different. This is a useful lesson for managers. Each of our roles gives us large territory to cover, and in most organizations, it is generally up to us to define all the boundaries involved. We can take the initiative to expand our roles, and contribute outside our day-jobs to cross-functional teams, even if in an area we don't know much about but like. It is up to us to put up our hands for a new assignment or project when the opportunity arises, thus constantly expanding our own intellectual territory.

Gender Diversity

Now, here is an unusual but relevant corporate gender lesson from the world of horses. Bands of horses are generally led by a dominant mare (a female horse). This is contrary to popular perception that a stallion (male horse) is the ruler of the herd. The mare leads the herd of horses to waterholes, and she also guides them to sheltered places out of the wind when winter storms howl. The mare gets this pride of place as leader of the herd because she is considered more mature and caring, more familiar with the terrain and resources available. There is clearly a gender lesson here for all of us to reflect on.

Don't Fool Around

On important matters, don't rely only on the office grapevine. You must get the truth from the horse's mouth. If you see your boss or colleagues trying to discuss or make meaningless changes to plans which have been agreed upon, do remind them not to change horses midstream. The most likely result of doing so is drowning.

If you are heading a big change management project, remember that you must work hard to convince all team members—you can take horses to water, but you can't make them drink.

If you are in a team which is handling important proprietary technology or commercially sensitive information, beware of a Trojan Horse in your midst. Be alert, and keep such information locked away at all times.

Sometimes light-hearted recreational activity is important to break the seriousness and monotony of the workplace. So, go ahead, indulge in some good natured horseplay from time to time.

I would like to remind all managers who evaluate their team members that champion horses are generally consistently high performers, but they don't necessarily win every race.

45

The New-Age Boss

A few unsolicited suggestions for bosses to consider.

A study of CEOs, published some time ago by Harvard Business School, reveals some shocking truths. These top bosses spend only 4 per cent of their day thinking about long-term strategy, according to the 'What Do CEOs Do?' Harvard working paper.

The study finds that these CEOs work for forty-eight hours a week but spend 60 per cent of that time in meetings—and we know what most meetings are like. They get bogged down in day-to-day operations, and they also feel they must dash around the world meeting clients (no doubt all this jet-setting makes them feel very important). To be fair, this Harvard working paper has only researched the CEOs of ninety-four Italian firms. But it might not be far from the truth in other parts of the world, including in India. So, given this unfortunate context, it is important to ask, what should bosses do? Here are some suggestions, all put forward with genuinely good intent.

Enhance Their Thought Process

To begin with, bosses should spend time thinking about the future of the business, about the office and about all of us. Yet, as we know all too well, bosses rarely do so. And when they eventually do get around to thinking briefly, they mostly arrive at the expensive conclusion that this cerebral activity should be delegated to management consultants. But many wise consultants try to figure out what the bosses are thinking, and then faithfully reflect these views in their recommendations. However, since the bosses aren't really thinking, the consultants present glossy 1,000-page reports containing nothing of substantial value. This leads to a period of absolutely zero thinking, except a general bemoaning of the top dollars spent on the consultants. To break out of this vicious cycle of emptiness, bosses should take time off to think—retire to the mountainsides or beaches while they are thinking, if they wish.

Let Employees Be

Having applied some thought and given us some (hopefully) useful directions, bosses should then leave us alone. A time-and-motion study of employees in modern offices is likely to show that staffers spend more time responding to bosses and attending endless meetings called by them than actually doing good work with a free and relaxed mind. Bosses are a significant cause of recurring hypertension, which we all agree does not help creative or productive work. So, our considered recommendation is that bosses and CEOs be given the full liberty of working from their far-off homes for at least two days a week, though we take no responsibility for the domestic discord this can potentially cause in their lives. We also recommend that bosses be encouraged to interact intensively and actively with their own bosses, including members of the board of directors and such worthies—this will engage their time productively and keep them off our backs.

Learn to Appreciate Staffers

Bosses should learn to stop by and promptly express their appreciation whenever they see a good intent, action or result. Indian managers are particularly poor at this sort of thing. Even when they get around to saying anything positive to their team members, they rarely go beyond a fleeting smile, a few mumbled words and a limp handshake. Our first recommendation is that we refresh our bosses' rather limited lexicon. They should know that words like 'brilliant', 'superlative', 'smashing' and 'wonderful' were created with a purpose. Our second recommendation is that CEOs or top bosses should hand out ten exciting gifts every month without fail for initiatives taken by their team members that they consider excellent. Because in any organization worth its top line and bottom line, there will certainly be at least ten positive things occurring every month. However, if these positive things are not happening in any month, then the head honcho may wish to consider a different plan of action—resigning with immediate effect.

Take Time Off, Lots of It

Bosses should take time off from work every now and then— in the interests of their own mental health, but primarily for the well-being of their teams. A boss just back from a holiday is a bright and friendly guy. In sharp contrast, a boss who has not taken a vacation for more than a year is generally a grumpy fellow, for he has not seen either sunshine or the skies, nor has he spent vacant time loitering. And business-related travel does not really count.

Teams can actively encourage such vacationing by sending their bosses alluring picture postcards of Caribbean beaches, Alaskan cruises and the snow-clad Alps. Even better, send a few of these pictures to his or her spouse as well. The last one is usually an effective intervention. Companies can actively help in this endeavour by ensuring that part of the annual variable pay for senior management is handed out as a mandatory one-week holiday package that cannot be exchanged for cash and lapses at the end of the year.

Learn to Relax and Smile

Nothing works better for all of us than bosses who know how to take it cool and relax. A smiling CEO is a rare but significant company asset. Bosses should be firm and focused, but they should also actively learn to take digs at themselves, take teams out to the movies and races, speak about interesting cabbages and assorted kings, be champion guzzlers and greedy eaters. For all this to happen, there is one important prerequisite—bosses need to understand that while growth, profitability, RoIs (returns on investment) and such grave, important metrics are necessary, they are not sufficient conditions for a team's happy success. On the other hand, an infectious laugh, the ability to contemplate the lighter side, to mimic and play along, to be easy-going when necessary, to chill out sometimes—these are the small things that matter hugely. Whether the going is easy or incredibly tough, bosses need to relax and smile.

My team members in office and my family fervently hope that I practise what I have preached in this essay.

46

Coffee, Matcha or Coconut Water?

Managers are increasingly known by the snacks and beverages they serve. Here is a guide.

There was a time, now in the distant past, when managers offered their guests a cup of milky tea and biscuits, served by a pantry boy. In most cases, the guests did not have a choice. You ate and drank what was served, which was generally full of sugar and cream, the sweeter the better. Sometimes, in fancier offices, sugar cubes were served separately on the side, and you could decide how many to empty into your system.

In today's new-age offices, all this has changed dramatically. The range of snacks and beverages now on offer is amazingly diverse. In fact, you can classify managers by what they serve you when you visit their offices. Conversely, therefore, your visitors are silently classifying you too, based on what you offer them. Therefore, it is important to understand this subject in greater depth, and this column offers you an introductory primer.

Green Tea Manager

This fitness-conscious manager will offer you tea and coffee, but will then nudge you to drink green tea. 'Green tea is most healthy for the heart,' he is likely to say, 'and you can have it without milk and sugar, which is good for you.' If you were looking forward to a hot cup of elaichi-flavoured, sugared masala chai, you won't be getting it here, because this man has read that sugar is the new tobacco, and he believes in great health for one and all. During long meetings, if a couple of cups of sugarless green tea have already worked their magic on your heart, you could take a break, go down to the chaiwallah outside, and drink your preferred chai.

Samosa Type

This person believes that late evening meetings must be accompanied by greasy samosas stuffed with aloo and mint chutney by the side, washed down with hot tea or coffee. So, if you are keen on eating such stuff, ensure that your meetings with him are scheduled around 6 p.m. or thereabouts. Unfortunately, this species of manager is fast disappearing in a fitness-obsessed world. Therefore, you must encourage the residual members of this clan by appreciating the samosa or kachori offered and even asking for a refill shamelessly. In all likelihood, he will join you in this encore.

Protein Dude

A number of executives have now concluded, rightly or wrongly, that they need lots of protein to survive the hectic pace of the corporate world. These protein dudes typically tend to be fitness freaks, with aspirations of a well-toned body. They are known to serve their visitors (and themselves) nuts of various types, because nuts are high in protein—peanuts and almonds are par for the course, and corner offices may also occasionally serve you expensive barbecue-flavoured cashew nuts and toasted walnuts. The problem with nuts is that you really cannot stop eating them, so it is important that you push away these addictive bowls after a while. Or simply ask the person next to you to pass them on down the table. Also, eat only one at a time and slowly, notwithstanding the temptation to munch quickly on multiple nuts together.

All-Natural Yogi

He (or she) believes in the power of natural ingredients and abhors everything that is even remotely processed or synthetic. Therefore, she is totally unlikely to serve you carbonated soft drinks, or even cookies with added processed sugar. So, what can you expect from this well-intentioned yogi? Coconut water, fresh sugarcane juice, kokum juice are interesting possibilities. I have known of managers who have begun serving their guests only slices of fresh fruit. Once, on a visit to a large corporation in China, I attended a long five-hour meeting with an all-natural Chinese yogi and his team, munching exclusively on a wide range of fruit, and drinking fresh jasmine-flavoured green tea which was constantly refilled. I must say this was a refreshing change, because five hours with cookies would have been impossible.

Coffee and Tea Connoisseur

This connoisseur manager believes that fine coffee and tea, like fine wine, are beautiful stories to be sipped and appreciated in their own right. She (or he) is, of course, keen to play a role in such evangelisation. So, he will offer you a choice between espresso, cappuccino and 'Monsoon Malabar Fresh Brewed' coffee. Or between matcha, redbush tea and 'First Flush Darjeeling'. You need to brush up on your beverage vocabulary before visiting this connoisseur or else you may end up ordering the wrong cup for yourself. For instance, robust and deep drinking people who are used to large mugs of coffee may feel disappointed when they receive a very small dollop of espresso in a small Italian-style cup. Also, be prepared to hear the connoisseur out, as he or she waxes eloquently on the flavours and tales of these coffees and teas. This is sometimes interesting, but could also turn out to be repetitive if you are meeting him or her often.

Badam Burfi Big Boss

This is the traditional Indian businessman manager at his hospitable best. He will offer his special guests the most exclusive snacks, totally Indian in their ethos—kaju katli, badam burfi, fried and peppered cashew nuts, rich dry fruit chivda mixtures, etc. on steel platters—you get the picture. Then, thick boiled tea, heavily flavoured with elaichi and ginger. An alternative on hot summer mornings will be shikanji or sweet lassi. All this will be followed by cloves and saunf, offered in small silver boxes, to help freshen your mouth after this hearty repast. The calorie gain from each such encounter is to be counted in millions, but these are snacks to die for and, believe me, they disappear very rapidly.

Local Hero

This is a son-of-the-soil manager, who believes his guests should eat and drink local specialities, to celebrate the cuisine of the land. So, in Mumbai, he will offer you vadapav and cutting chai. In Chennai, handmade kai murukku and filter coffee. In Bengaluru, there is the possibility of mini rava idlis and mysorepak. In Delhi, who knows, but be very careful. These heroes may progress to higher levels of sophistication by offering local foods with a fusion twist, such as kheema vada pav (which is delicious) or rava idlis with a hint of wasabi (handle with caution, they go sharp into your head in no time). An interesting change from biscuits and sandwiches, but be prepared for hot and spicy stuff.

I always offer my visitors a cool glass of water, and I wish that ice cream were served more often in corporate offices because it is healthy and delicious.

47

What Should You Do When You Fly?

How executives can make the most of their hours in the air.

Managers are flying more than ever before. Each year, several million hours of business travel are clocked by energetic executives travelling busily to client locations and conferences, and tired managers flying back home at the end of a tough day. How should managers utilize these many long hours in the air to maximize professional growth and happiness?

Typically, busy executives use flights to catch up on sleep or read the newspaper. Many attempt to work on their laptop computers, notwithstanding the cramped yogic posture that this requires, amidst narrow economy class seats. These have become virtually automatic flying habits. But have you thoughtfully considered many other nice and useful things that you can do while flying?

One important thing that executives need to realize is that flying time is 'me-time'. This is very valuable space and time for yourself, up in the air—an invaluable window of calm in today's hectic world, where managers are constantly balancing the demands of bosses, clients, teams and family. Therefore, maximizing the use of flying time for yourself is important. Here are some interesting things you can consider doing.

Quiet Meditation

A flight is a brilliant place to meditate. After take-off, tell the crew not to disturb you. Then, use any meditation technique which you have taken a fancy for. Close your eyes and breathe deeply, do your best to banish all distracting thoughts from your smart managerial mind. If you are a digital geek, use a meditation app. If you are merely musically oriented, carry some meditative chanting or music on your smartphone, and plug into it. In olden times, people used to go high up to the Himalayas to meditate. Think of flights as modern Himalayan caves, soaring well above earth. There is something about flying 30,000 feet high up in the skies, that naturally promotes the meditative spirit.

Joy of Eating

Flights can become great eating places, particularly if you bring your own favourite food. At airports, I often pick up the comfort food I love (e.g., fried chicken or a tuna sandwich), and then I eat it, slowly and totally undisturbed, on board my flights. This is an amazingly happy pastime because eating your favourite meal slowly, with absolutely no upcoming urgent meetings or digital distractions, is suddenly so liberating. You focus totally on the food you love, and experience delicious flavours which you have taken for granted. Given that many executives eat their daily meals hastily, sandwiched between hectic meetings, relaxed eating on flights is a thoroughly rejuvenating activity. Believe me.

Deep Reflection

Use the uninterrupted time you get on flights to reflect deeply on your work and life. As managers, we are often addicted to action, leaving ourselves very little time for reflection. Flying time can provide us the answer. Pull out your notebook, list out everything that is going superbly for you and things that are not going so well, then ask yourself all the searching questions. Reflect on what you can do better, at office and home, over the next several days and weeks. Reflect on the higher purpose of your career or life, that's important too. Aircrafts are particularly good places for such thinking sessions because you are far away from the hurly-burly of daily life, and good reflection requires distance from the battleground.

Spontaneous Conversation

Flights are wonderful places to strike up conversations with strangers, which can often turn out to be insightful. Once, I spoke to a young chef seated next to me, and in two hours, I had obtained delightful insights into how customized menus are created for big, fat weddings. On another occasion, I spoke to a portly businessman, who took me on a very interesting voyage through the joys and sorrows of the real estate business, with a remarkable interlude on why and how he always ends up extending his holidays in Goa. Serendipitous conversations with strangers enable you to break away from the same few people you meet each day, and so they add a fresh dimension to your life.

Total Binge-Watching

What better place to binge-watch Netflix or unwind over your favourite movies than on a long flight? Binge-watching is becoming a cultural phenomenon of our times, and if done in moderation, it helps you unwind totally from daily pressures, and have super fun with some great content. Binge-watching by yourself at home or office can potentially have varying adverse impacts, including deteriorating relationships and letters of warning. However, on a flight, there is no such guilt at all because you are alone and this is your personal time.

Time to Create

A flight provides you uninterrupted space and time for any creative activity that you love. This could include writing a thought paper for an interesting project that has been on your mind, sketching a design or doodling, creating a collage of photographs on your computer, creatively planning your next holiday or building imaginative ideas for your next team offsite. Some of my best ideas and writings have taken birth on flights, and creative pursuits are always energizing.

I am always keen to engage in an interesting conversation on a flight, but only after I have eaten well.

48

New Principles of Our Office Lives

Here are some laws that govern our modern workplaces.

Many decades ago, Parkinson's Law entered the world of management. This famous law, discovered by C. Northcote Parkinson, simply said that work expands to fill the time available for its completion. The law remains unchanged after many years, and so many of us continue to struggle with the phenomenon of ever-expanding work.

Much water has flown under rickety corporate bridges since the discovery of this very important principle. It is now time, we think, to consider many new important laws that have seeped into our modern offices since then. Reflecting on these principles will make executives more sensitive to the real issues that underpin our office lives. Here is a primer which I hope you enjoy and internalize.

Occam's PowerPoint Principle

This is one of the most productive modern principles of our age. It states that any meaningful presentation can be reduced to a maximum of ten slides. Of course, this requires lots of thinking to decide what the essential core of the presentation is, and a harsh delete button on every slide that does not serve this purpose. The converse of this principle states that the longer a presentation is, the less it is worth your time. And if the presentation exceeds around thirty slides, it is best to skip it. Apply this principle in your own presentations, and watch the jump in productivity and happiness all around. This principle is named in tribute to Occam, the philosopher who urged economy in everything, and famously said—'It is futile to do with more things any act which can be done with fewer.'

Gayatri's Millennials Law

This law simply states that, if you are an adult manager (like me), you can never discover what millennials in your office really want, however much you search for the truth. So much has been written on what inspires millennials, what puts them off, what kind of work they like to do, what they know and what they desire. It turns out that lots of this is guesswork by millennial watchers who are generally adults, and the rest frequently changes because millennials themselves constantly evolve. If you don't agree, speak to a few millennials, and we can discuss the after-effects after you have recovered somewhat from your encounters. This law is named after the millennial whom I think I know best, but then frequently discover that I am totally wrong about—my daughter Gayatri.

Alice in Digital Wonderland Rule

This rule postulates that in any meeting, at least one participant is constantly in a digital wonderland. Of course, with the plethora of digital distractions—email, WhatsApp, Facebook, etc.—around us and our ubiquitous mobile phones with us all the time, this rule will come as no surprise. In fact, in most meetings there will not be just one person, but multiple people who are avid followers of this rule, busy on their digital devices. If this irritates you, and you have the required powers, you could consider the harsh but necessary counter-rule of requesting participants to put away their mobile phones during meetings. There will be some grumbling, but a digital detox helps.

MBAs' Law of Jargon

This law, dedicated to countless MBAs like myself, states that jargon will be generously used by managers who have been to business school. It goes on to state that there are several levels of jargon, which MBAs will progressively master during their illustrious careers. Now, jargon may be used for very different purposes. For instance, to create high-sounding statements of vision or strategy, or to say something where there is very little to be said, or to obfuscate the truth. An immediate corollary of this law is that all executives have to learn to cut through the jargon in their offices, and understand what any official statement really, truly means. Another useful corollary to bear in mind is that simple sentences and speeches which clearly convey their meaning stand out for being rare, and are therefore greatly appreciated.

The Friday Evening Principle

This rather uncomfortable principle states that there is always a high probability of urgent work or extensive reading material landing on your table or in your inbox on a Friday evening, just as you are planning to leave for the weekend. The root cause of this principle is that urgency does not respect weekends, and neither do many managers. Yet another reason is that most executives tend to finish their major project for the week on a Friday afternoon, and then promptly email their output to other team members, such as yourself, for review and comments. The only antidote to this principle is to work very hard and smart during the week, and also have a well-understood no-work-on-weekends rule in offices, to be broken only in case of real emergencies.

The General Theory of Entropy

This is the most general of modern office principles, shamelessly borrowed from the theories of thermodynamics. It postulates that all our office accessories—work tables, computers, mobile phones, bags that we carry—will tend towards entropy, as they constantly gather more paper, more email, more apps and more documents. This will inevitably result in our tables being overloaded by mountains of paper, computers groaning under the weight of unread documents, and bags or office backpacks gaining weight even faster than executives do. In this glorious Information Age, where ever-expanding bodies of knowledge constantly and steadily stream into our lives, the only reprieve from this law is to retain just the barest minimum information required, and destroy or delete everything else immediately and ruthlessly. A clean desk is, of course, the holy grail that we can all aim for.

I am a fervent believer in Harish's law of simplicity, which I named after myself, in a moment of conceit. This law states that corporate life should be kept really simple through hard work, thoughtful but sharp decisions, and positive, straightforward relationships.

49

Taking Note of What Is Said

The six kinds of note-takers you will find at meetings, from the doodler to the digital geek.

We keep notes throughout our lives. As students, we take down lectures, making sure we don't miss anything important. Then, as we enter corporate life, we realize that keeping notes of what is said at the numerous meetings we attend is important too.

Keeping good notes can have a significant impact on the results we achieve at the workplace—because some of the points we note down can actually prompt us to act. No wonder that note-keeping in office has evolved into an art, with managers developing their own methods. This corporate artform requires due attention, therefore I bring you here some of the most popular styles of keeping notes so that you can reflect on, and finetune, your own style.

Long-Form Essayist

This manager carries a large notebook around and writes copious notes on every single thing that is discussed in meetings. Open their notebook, and you will find essays documenting what each person said, with some sections underlined for effect. This style generally works well for managers who have to summarize the proceedings of meetings. For most others, it does not work, because long essays are not easy to read. However, taking down such extensive notes ensures that you are perceived as someone who is deeply invested in the meeting, which may win you some brownie points.

Doodler

The doodler stands in direct contrast to the long-form essayist. He carries a notebook, alright, but also carries a core belief that most of what is said in meetings is really a waste of time. So, he keeps himself busy during these discussions by doodling in his notebook. Occasionally, he may lazily scribble a note or two as well, if he hears something that sparks his interest. There is research indicating that doodling opens up your mind during meetings and makes you more creative, so don't rule this out as a useless pursuit.

Laptop Scribe

The laptop scribe does not believe in ancient devices such as a paper and pen. He always walks into meetings armed with his laptop. More often than not, this is a sleek Mac or a fancy Microsoft Surface. As soon as the meeting commences, he promptly opens his laptop and begins furiously typing notes. The laptop screen creates a nice barrier between himself and everyone else at the meeting, so you cannot really make out whether he is taking notes, answering email or browsing Facebook. Thus, this style confers multiple advantages on the notetaker, apart from ensuring that he has all the notes digitally captured and ready to email out to others, immediately after the meeting.

Digital Geek

The digital geek goes far beyond the laptop scribe, in his effortless embrace of cool technology. For him or her, even laptops and word processors are terribly outdated devices. Instead, he uses apps designed specifically for note-keeping, all on his smartphone with a large screen, with a sleek black stylus. You will find him using customized apps such as Simplenote, Evernote, Google Keep and many other 'app-ropriate' note-taking tools. He will wax eloquent on how these apps add not just to his notes, but also to his overall sense of being part of a connected planet. To see this style in action, look out for technology evangelists and millennials.

Little Black Notebook

This impressive person carries a little black notebook in the pocket of his shirt or jacket. He is a precise person who believes in extreme brevity, and only in points that require his own thought or action. When he comes across a specific point being made that requires noting down, he whips out this tiny notebook, jots it down immediately and puts the book back in his pocket. I have noticed that these notebooks are curiously always black in colour. This style is generally adopted by people who consider themselves no-nonsense managers with a strong bias for action.

Moleskine Dude

Here is a manager who believes that the quality of the notebook is as important as the quality of the notes themselves. He or she will only carry branded notebooks such as the Moleskine, the elegant variety originally used by creative geniuses such as Van Gogh and Ernest Hemmingway. Other exotic brands include Leuchtturm1917, Rhodia or Mont Blanc. The hope here is that the interesting story and rich feel of the notebook rubs off positively on your creative side, leading to notes and jottings that can eventually amaze everyone.

I carry a ruled school notebook everywhere, note down whatever I consider important and worry perennially that I may lose this book.

50

How Do You Look during Meetings?

A guide to how managers can be classified by their looks in conference rooms.

Managers can be classified in many conventional ways—based on their functional expertise, performance, potential, gender, qualifications and age. Our HR teams are experts at classifications, but most of these methods miss the point because they don't measure how engaged the manager is with his or her workplace. On the other hand, an excellent method of measuring how connected managers are with their workplaces is to classify them by how they look during a meeting. By 'look' I don't mean how managers dress or preen themselves, though that carries a lot of meaning too. I mean how managers actually look and behave during a meeting.

Since there are no known scientific studies on this important aspect of our workplaces, this column is a guide to classifying managers by their looks during meetings, for your easy reference. When you find yourself in a meeting next time, try to mentally classify your colleagues using this guide. This will give you new insights into your team, which can be fun.

Eager Listener

The Eager Listener is all ears to what the boss is saying during a meeting. He (or she) doesn't want to miss a single word and is most anxious that he should not lose out on any pearls of wisdom which may roll by on the conference table. During all meetings he resembles a picture of total concentration, looking and listening with eyes and ears wide open, and faithfully writing down everything that the boss says. He fills reams of pages with his detailed notes, leaving many of us to often wonder whether we are missing out on any important stuff. Sometimes, you can even hear him say—'Boss, that was an excellent point, can you repeat it once more for me?' Mr Eager Listener is there to learn, and to impress the boss with his listening skills. Don't ever disturb him when the session is on.

Deep Thinker

The Thinker has a faraway look at meetings. The impression you get is that he is reflecting deeply on the proceedings, on everything that has been said until now. He never writes because he believes in absorbing everything directly into his deep and capacious mind. Sometimes, his eyes are even closed. Now, don't make the mistake of thinking that they are catching a siesta during a boring session—the closed eyes actually indicate meditative reflection, and signal a highly evolved manager who absorbs only the truths and shuts out all the noise. Sometimes such deep thinking is accompanied by gentle snoring, at which point you should silently prod this colleague, at the risk of interrupting his train of silent thought.

Nodding Head

This look is popular amongst many managers. They keep nodding their heads during meetings, mostly without saying anything. Of course, there are different varieties of nods, which you need to recognize. One sort of nod, up and down, signals agreement with what is being said. Another nod, sideways, signals some degree of disagreement. Some nods, which go both upwards and sideways, are confusing in their intent. Nods can be rapid, or slow, conveying very different things. Sometimes, these managers will seek out their friends and allies in the meeting room, look at them, nod and smile. Nods enable managers to silently convey their views, without taking the risk of standing up and speaking. The Nodding Head is an engaged manager, but one who also believes in harmony and smooth progress of the meeting.

Digital Networker

This manager has a digital sort of look on his face throughout meetings, because he is always waiting for an opportunity to scroll through his mobile phone again. He believes that he is capable of multitasking with ease, that a little bit of texting or emailing or WhatsApp-ing will never distract him from the discussion at hand. He may occasionally make a comment or an observation, to show everyone how focused he is on the content of the meeting. It is unlikely though that he will add much real value to the meeting, because his thoughts are mostly drifting in cyberspace. You will see him smile or frown, but this is based on the content of the latest digital message he has received, and not what is happening in the meeting itself. The digital networker generally has harmless intent and a very low attention span, but he can be terribly distracting to others, and of course he is very disengaged.

Impatient Watchman

Here is a manager who feels the meeting is a total waste of his time, or is dragging on for too long, and is constantly looking down at his wristwatch. He looks at his watch when he comes into the conference room, and he then consults it from time to time. It is likely that he may ask everyone to do a time-check, at some point during the meeting. While all this activity does not make time go any faster, it indicates to everyone else in the room that the Impatient Watchman will soon leave. When he eventually leaves the meeting on the dot of the hour after one final look at his watch, his expression says it all—Guys, I know how to keep to my time, and many of you don't. In India, where many of our meetings drag on for too long, we can learn something from him.

Distinguished Observer

This is the most intriguing type of look, and often difficult to read. This person sits through the entire meeting with great poise, but never once contributes to the proceedings. Sometimes he wears a haughty, disdainful look, as if the subject of the meeting is beneath him. At other times, you will see an inscrutable look on his face. Often, a forbidding look too, which ensures that no one else in the meeting conjures up the courage to speak with him. Unlike the impatient watchman, he is no hurry to leave. You wonder why he is there, and what he is up to. All this adds to the general sense of intrigue. In simple truth, he may have failed to understand anything said during the meeting. But he could also be an alien, or a disinterested individual, or he could be a man who has come into the meeting entirely by mistake. After all, we have all types in our offices, as you know.

I think the best way to look good at meetings is to keep your ears and mind open at all times, but to open your mouth only when you have something new and relevant to say.

Epilogue

The last word

A license I enjoy as an author is the right to always have the last word, at least in the epilogue. Of course, the final say regarding the book is that of the readers. I hope it will be a kind word, but I will have to await the reviews to know for sure.

Office-goers would be concerned with a more relevant question: who gets to have the last say in our offices? Now, this is a very interesting question, with many possible answers.

In some cases, the boss gets the last word. She often calls the meeting to a finish by saying something like, 'Thank you, guys, that was a very good discussion. Now let's get going with the action points we've talked about.' Thus leaving the action-ball entirely in our hands, hopefully for a free kick into the goal.

Or, God forbid, the boss may even say something like 'This is such a terrible meeting. I am stopping this discussion right here because none of you are really prepared.' And then he may storm off for lunch, while all of us look at each other in silent commiseration.

In a few other cases, the most impatient person gets the last word. They may bring the meeting to an end by telling us: 'Now, we've been here for three hours. Isn't that enough, guys? Let's leave before everything shuts down.'

Occasionally, the person who makes everything shut down in office gets the last word. He could be the electrician or office assistant who shuts off the office air-conditioners promptly at 6 p.m. each day. The air in the conference room soon gets stifling (if the conversation has not made it stuffy enough already), and then everyone gets up slowly and starts leaving.

Sometimes, the last word belongs to the boss's spouse, who may be far away from office but telephones during a meeting to remind him that their darling daughter is performing at the school programme that begins in exactly half an hour. Would the boss mind leaving office immediately to attend the event? Because what is more important—an event for which your daughter has rehearsed meticulously for an entire month, or one more stupid meeting in your office? The answer becomes immediately obvious to everyone in the room.

On video calls, the last word may belong to someone in the far-off corporate headquarters of Zoom, particularly if you are using a free version of the software which imposes strict limits on timing. The call simply shuts down, forcing the meeting to an abrupt and premature conclusion. Everyone then sits looking at their laptop or mobile screens gone blank. In some dire circumstances, a new video meeting is convened in a few minutes, to continue with the business at hand. Hence the last word is not really the last word, if you know what I mean.

Notwithstanding these infinite possibilities, we all wish to have at least some defining say regarding our immediate workspaces and office practices. Making our workplaces more productive and happier spaces is important for us, regardless of our hierarchical levels or formal powers of authority because we live in our offices for so many hours every day, so many days of the year.

I'm no different and wanted to get in a word or two on the business of living and working in offices. And so, the essays in this book. I love observing people and from many years of accumulated observation, I thought I developed some understanding into what leads to better work and happier teams in our offices. These writings became a conduit through which I could share some of these insights and begin some discussion.

Often, as I stepped back to observe, I was seized by the humour that percolates so many work situations, and therefore the need for us office people to take ourselves less seriously. Good work demands our serious attention, of course. But happy offices also require levity and fun. Hence the light and irreverent tone you may have noticed in many parts of this book.

Mint provided me with opportunity to write for a column where I could publish these pieces quite regularly. I have enjoyed writing for this wonderful newspaper, and this also gave me the right to call myself a columnist. I must confess that I secretly enjoyed this entitlement, because it is quite nice and sometimes even fashionable to be called so. At some parties, it would even fetch me an extra glass of wine.

However, in choosing this path, I had to agree that my editor would have the right to shape the final version of each article. In other words, my editor would have the last word, and not me.

So, as you will see, except for the privilege of writing epilogues in my books, such as this one, I have rarely had the last word. This brings me quite naturally to a final office secret which I wish to share with all of you—that getting the last word in is one of the most difficult things in life, regardless of whether you are a manager in a company, a columnist with a newspaper or a lawyer in a law firm.

Therefore, whenever you get the opportunity, please do not miss it. For instance, if you wish to have the last word about this book, it's really very simple. All you have to do is to write to me at bhatharish@hotmail.com.

Acknowledgements

I constantly think about the human truths that shape our workplaces because I have spent over thirty-five years of my life in offices doing various things, mainly working, I would like to think, but also laughing, crying, talking, eating, drinking, worrying, celebrating, travelling, making presentations, cleaning out my desk, Zoom calling, falling asleep, emailing and texting.

Across all these myriad workplace activities, my learnings on what makes offices tick well have come primarily from my colleagues. I acknowledge the invaluable role that my bosses, team members, peers and friends have played in helping me discover the office secrets that I have narrated in this book.

My sincere thanks to many of my colleagues who taught me that while we should work hard with complete dedication to the tasks at hand, we should never take ourselves too seriously. The ability to laugh at ourselves is such an important part of discovering ourselves and some of the workplace secrets that really matter. This has led to my fledgling attempts at humour which flow through many of the essays in this book.

I would like to thank the Tata Group, where I have worked for all these three decades and more, for providing me such a wonderful professional home. It has been a privilege being part of this timeless institution. The Tata workplaces which I have been part of—in companies as diverse as Tata Tea, Titan and Tata Sons—have nurtured my thinking and my approach to office life. The Tata Group has also consistently encouraged me in my pursuit of writing, alongside my work as a marketer, for which I am truly grateful.

I would like to acknowledge the exemplary support and inputs I have received from the editor of the 'Business of Life' pages in the *Mint* newspaper, where most of these pieces were first published. I still recall that lazy Sunday evening in 2010 when I received an email from Priya Ramani, the then editor of *Mint Lounge*, informing me that she would like to publish my article on how people eat cookies in office. I was elated, and I ate a couple of cashew cookies to celebrate. This is how my journey as a columnist for this newspaper began.

Thereafter, for many years, Seema Chowdhry at *Mint* was my editor and she nurtured my writing with a lot of care. Over the past few years, Shalini Umachandran and Pooja Singh have provided me all the guidance and encouragement required. They have been patient with me and their editing has taught me several lessons in the art of succinct, clear writing. I have enjoyed my weekend telephone calls with them to discuss the theme of each forthcoming article. Thank you so much, Seema, Shalini and Pooja.

While developing many of these articles, I have turned to a wonderful colleague and friend, Suparna Mitra, who thinks deeply about people and teams. Suparna and I worked together in the Titan Company for many years, and we have kept in constant touch thereafter. Despite her hectic schedules as CEO of the watches and wearables business of Titan, she has always been generous in providing me with her time and thoughts. Thanks a lot, Suparna.

To Milee Ashwarya at Penguin Random House, my grateful thanks for believing in me, and being such a strong supporter of writing. When I called Milee to put forward a proposal for this book, she not just took the time to hear me out but also engaged in a detailed spontaneous discussion about the theme. We went on to talk about how best the book could appeal and add value to readers. That conversation was the foundation on which this book was built. Milee's well-honed instinct for what can potentially make a book very successful is worth its weight in gold.

Dipanjali Chadha, my editor for this book, deserves credit and applause for whipping the manuscript into shape. She wielded her editor's pen clinically and with great precision, but she also took care to explain to me why each change was necessary. Dipanjali was also very patient with me as we worked our way through the title, the design of the cover page and so many other matters of detail which go into the crafting of a good book.

Manali Das, who has copyedited the book, has ensured that every phrase and line flows beautifully and correctly. Her understanding of the nuances of the English language has helped refine the text significantly.

My thanks are also due to the entire team at Penguin Random House, which has helped design, develop and publish this book.

My mother, Jayanthi, is a writer at heart, and she has always encouraged me to write. She used to write an occasional column, many years ago, for a Kannada magazine. I think this inspired me to begin writing for newspapers when I was in higher secondary school. My books feature on her bedside, and she has been quite candid with me regarding which of my writings she likes and the ones she dislikes. Her blessings have provided me with great strength as I worked on this book.

My daughter, Gayatri, has also constantly encouraged me to pursue my writing. She is an avid reader and also a fierce critic. I am hoping that this book will get her approval.

My wife, Veena, has read each essay in this book before it was first published in the *Mint* newspaper. Her initial comments would inevitably be critical. While some of her tough observations were difficult for me to digest, they eventually helped me improve and hone these writings. For the essays and stories contained in this book, she also brought to bear her own perspectives on the workplace, which are often quite different from mine. Her work as a data scientist in a global company provides her a wonderful window into working with people from various diverse cultures across the world. She would discuss some of these experiences and learnings with me from time to time, and I think they have got seamlessly woven into many of these articles. At home, Veena has created the warm, positive and peaceful environment and space required for me to write. I am so happy that she has chosen to be my companion in life. Her active encouragement and support have been such a strong foundation for my journey as an author. This is my home secret, which supplements all the office secrets in this book.

For me, writing is a great passion and a positive addiction. I thank God Almighty for blessing me with the capability and the urge to write. I pray to Saraswati, the Goddess of Knowledge, to bless me with the gifts of knowledge and writing for the rest of my life.

Notes

The fifty articles included in this book were originally published in the *Mint* newspaper, on the dates given below. They were published in this newspaper in a column titled 'Tongue-in-cheek'—a name which reflected the irreverent and light-hearted tone of many of these pieces. The first such column appeared in February 2010, and the articles have appeared at fairly regular intervals thereafter, each piece revealing an office secret that has been on my mind.

1. Why Do People Talk So Much during Meetings? (22 August 2022)
2. Why Being Generous Is an Essential Trait of a Great Leader (27 June 2022)
3. The Cookie Club (21 February 2010)
4. Six Rules That Marked Working from Home (4 March 2022)
5. Tired of Being Tired? Go Ahead, Hit the Refresh Button (28 February 2022)

6. Have You Spotted the Balloon in Your Office? (20 February 2023)

7. Why Daydreaming Is a Good Thing (4 October 2021)

8. Why Writing Makes Us Happier (25 July 2021)

9. A Beginner's Guide to Recovering from Meetings (10 December 2021)

10. Dump the Slides; Add Power to Your Point (12 November 2019)

11. The New Laws of the Digital Workplace (25 July 2019)

12. Your Office Companion Spills the Beans (2 September 2021*)

13. Do You Ask Questions That Really Matter? (25 March 2019)

14. Make February Your New January (3 February 2019)

15. Listening: A Vital Managerial Skill (25 March 2018)

16. Pandemic Habits We Should Stick to (22 December 2021)

17. Tune into the Blues to Work Smart (1 September 2021*)

18. Finding Hotspots for Ideas (1 September 2021*)

19. What Your Wall Says about You on a Video Call (27 August 2021)

20. The Joy of Using a Notebook (11 February 2021)

21. Hercule Poirot Can Solve Your Work Problems, Too (12 November 2020)

22. Please Add Kindness to Your To-Do List as Well (24 September 2020)

23. Old-School Charm at Work (17 February 2013)

24. What If Working from Home Goes on Forever? (9 July 2020)

25. Seven Habits of Very Happy Managers (18 November 2012)

26. What the Dickens? (12 February 2012)

27. An Office Worker's Guide to the Zodiac (8 January 2012)
28. How Often Do You Praise Others? (16 January 2023)
29. Conference 101—and Ways to Add Some Fun (2 October 2011)
30. Monsters Inc. (14 August 2011)
31. The Geronimo Effect at Work (15 May 2011)
32. And the Office Oscar Goes To . . . (7 March 2011)
33. PERM Yourself in Office (29 June 2014)
34. Mathematics at Work (31 August 2014)
35. Meet Shakespeare, the Manager's Guru (28 December 2014)
36. Become a JEDI (8 October 2015)
37. Einstein on the Job (31 January 2016)
38. What to Wear, When (19 May 2015)
39. For Your Next Offsite, Opt for Offbeat Destinations (2 September 2021*)
40. The Art of ACE-ing Your Office Conversations (2 September 2021*)
41. SOAR above the Job (2 September 2021*)
42. Time to Think (30 July 2017)
43. What Your Cubicle Says about You (4 June 2017)
44. Horseplay at Work (23 March 2014)
45. The New-Age Boss (10 July 2011)
46. Coffee, Matcha or Coconut Water? (2 September 2021*)
47. What Should You Do When You Fly? (2 September 2021*)
48. New Principles of Our Office Lives (10 September 2017)
49. Taking Note of What Is Said (2 September 2021*)
50. How Do You Look during Meetings? (21 August 2016)

Legend: (*) – updated date as per online edition of *Mint*